SEXY
LITTLE KNITS

SEXY
LITTLE KNITS

CHIC DESIGNS TO KNIT AND CROCHET

Ashley Paige

PHOTOGRAPHY BY YU TSAI

POTTER
CRAFT

NEW YORK

Published in the United States by
Potter Craft, an imprint of the
Crown Publishing Group, a division
of Random House, Inc., New York.
www.crownpublishing.com
www.clarksonpotter.com

POTTER CRAFT and CLARKSON N. POTTER are
trademarks, and POTTER and colophon are
registered trademarks of Random House, Inc.

Library of Congress Cataloging-in-Publication
Data is available

ISBN 0-307-23657-9

Printed in the United States

Design by Chalkley Calderwood Pratt
Pattern Editing by Bobbie Summers
Photography by Yu Tsai

10 9 8 7 6 5 4 3 2 1

First Edition

This book is dedicated to my mom and my dad
— my thanks to them for the early memories
I will forever hold dear to my heart.

CONTENTS

ACKNOWLEDGMENTS

I would like to thank the following people for their help compiling the patterns and knitting the designs in this book:

REVOLUTIONARY KNITTERS
Herssik Avakian—V-neck sweater dress; Martha Blunt—winter tank; Magdalena Garcia—hippie halter top & tie bottom, silver glam crochet halter bikini, blue suede bikini, mesh one-piece, cap-sleeve mesh tank, drawstring cover, hemp V-neck top, heart babydoll halter dress, sexpot cami, sexpot bottom; Lyndsay Kane—little mermaid strapless top; Lesley Savin—winter panty, bathing beauty robe; Rie Sawai—winter panty; Bobbie Summers—bandeau butterfly crochet bikini, tiny halter tie bikini, terry short-shorts, racing-stripe terry jumper, cozy sleeper, sexpot cami; Shanita Williams—ribbon-yarn flared mini.

ASSISTANT DESIGNER
Rie Sawai

EXECUTIVE PATTERN EDITOR
Bobbie Summers

TECHNICAL EDITOR
Pat Harste

Special thanks to the following individuals for all their creativity and hard work compiling the photography in this book:

PHOTOGRAPHS & PRODUCTION
Chief Photographer—Yu Tsai
Assistant Photographer—Massimo Campana
Producer—Brandon Menchen
Photographer for images on pp. 89-93—Linda Serbu

HAIR & MAKEUP
Torsten Witte, www.torstenwitte.com

STYLISTS
Linda Serbu
Veronica Knight

Thanks also to my gorgeous models and where applicable, the agencies that represent them:

MODELS
Taylor Benning; Brittany—Photogenics; Camille—Nous Model Management; Carolina D'Amore—Nous Model Management; Harmony Ellington; Luba—Photogenics; Melissa Tellez; Anneca Peoples—Ford Models; Sonja; Jonelle Shirtcliff—M Management

Finally, thanks to Addi Needles for supplying all of the knitters who worked on this book with Addi Turbo Needles, "the fast needle with the natural touch."

Some of my friends' hip moms at the apartment complex where we lived in the '70s.

My mom on one of our family camping trips at the beach.

My mom (far right), her best friend, and me in a vacation beach house.

Me and a few of my favorite things: the ocean, a bikini, and sun.

INTRODUCTION

I grew up in the country and lived with my grandmother for many of my childhood years. She raised me on country music, biscuits, and gravy. Granny was a traditional homemaker who did everything from churning her own butter to sewing our clothes—she even crocheted all the Christmas ornaments for our tree and made beautiful quilts for every season.

When I revisit these memories of my grandmother, I understand why I'm so fascinated with handmade, beautiful things: she taught me to appreciate the patience, love, and devotion that go into every piece.

Today—although my lifestyle is more modern—I am a lot like my grandmother. I, too, believe in the beauty of the homemade; in fact, I have built my own business producing handmade knit clothing that is sold around the world. And although the inspiration came from her, as you will see, my designs are not Granny's, that's for sure!

In this book, I share some of my most successful knit bikini designs from the fashion runway as well as some brand-new clothing designs. After all, why shouldn't your knitting be fit for a celebrity?

The first chapter, "Peace, Love & Bikinis," is about my signature product: the sexy knit bikini! I've included patterns for a couple of crochet and knit styles in fabulous faux-suede yarn as well as a mesh lace-up-the-front one-piece. There's also a pattern for a super sexy butterfly-stitched bandeau with an "undie-" cut bottom to match, and a detailed hippie halter–style bikini with braided crisscross ties. All the swimwear patterns are hip and stylish enough to wear out after a day at the beach, but some of the recommended yarns are not ocean-, pool-, or hot tub–proof. Like many of the sweetest things in life, they're meant to look gorgeous rather than to withstand hard use. I've suggested yarn substitutions for those of you who like to swim, but keep in mind that knit bathing suits work better on land than in the water.

The second chapter, "Sunshine, Good Vibes," features vintage-style patterns inspired by the heyday of knit clothing—the '70s! Get ready to knit these cute short-shorts and hippie halters, terry-yarn jumpers, strapless tops, a darling heart-stitched sundress, a crocheted micromini in ribbon yarn, and hemp finger-weight yarn tops that would have been perfect for Woodstock!

The third chapter, "Cozy Homebodies," is full of soft, sensual knits for lazy days lounging around the house or for romantic evenings cuddling in front of the fireplace with your honey. A soft cashmere sleeper, winter mohair panties, and a see-through sexpot camisole are red-hot evidence that knitting is sexy!

If you share my love of handmade things and my desire to take the old-fashioned art of knitting into the modern world of hip fashion, grab your tiny needles, open your heart, and be revolutionary!

Peace, love, and sexy knitting!
—Ashley Paige

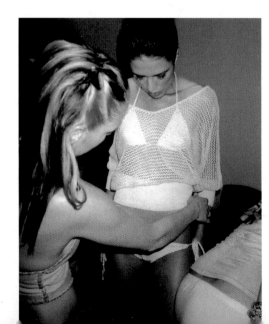

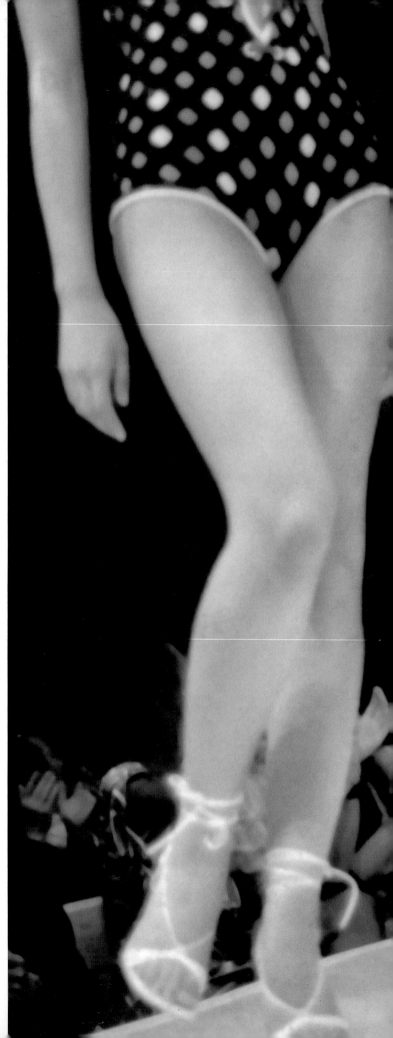

This was my first fashion show ever. It was an all-knit collection, and the media loved it.

SUGGESTIONS FOR SUBSTITUTING YARN

Yarn companies are well aware of the competitive advantage of carrying trendy novelty yarns. Therefore, they regularly discontinue wonderful yarns to update their collections with the more current styles that are driving the trends in the knitting industry. Because we used many of these specialty yarns to make the garments in this book, some of the yarns we recommend may not be available as the seasons pass and yarn stores stock new inventory. Don't panic—you'll almost certainly be able to find something even better and more fashionable. Just look for the same yarn weight and fiber content when selecting a substitute, and make sure you can maintain the same gauge specified in the pattern. If you can't find something suitable, ask a sales associate in your local yarn store for a recommendation. (Yarn shop staff members are notoriously enthusiastic and knowledgeable about what they sell.)

I don't recommend 100% cotton yarn for swimwear because it will soak up too much water and cause your suit to sag and stretch. Rayon dries quickly and will feel light on the body. Berroco Metallic FX yarn is a good choice; it's 85% rayon and 15% metallic. Viscose-blend or rayon-blend yarn can also be a good substitute if you really want to put your bikini to use in the water.

If you do substitute yarn, you will need to reswatch and make sure the new yarn produces the same gauge as the one recommended in the pattern.

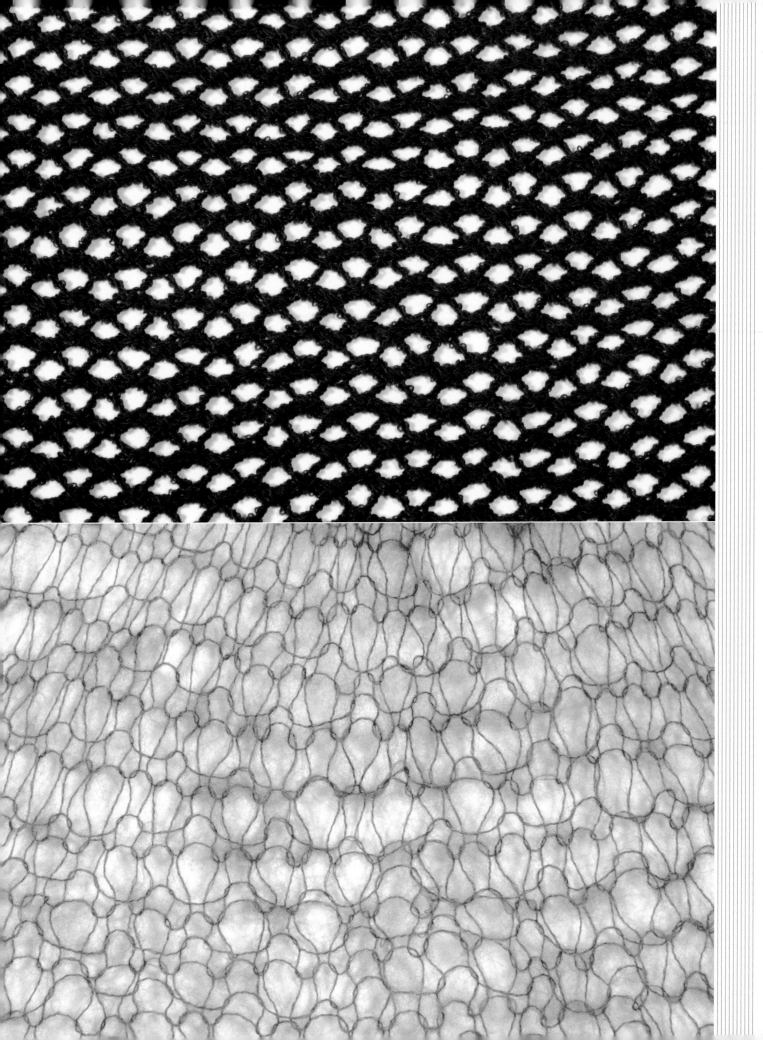

CHAPTER 1

PEACE, LOVE & BIKINIS

I live in Southern California, surrounded by the ocean, the sand, the surf, and the sun. It was only natural that when I combined my love of handcrafted, handmade designs with my love of the beach, I came up with . . . the knit bikini! What a look—I love its organic feel and its timeless wearability. It's got the sexiness of fishnet stockings, the femininity of lace, and the textural beauty of shells, eyelets, and mesh. Countless bombshells over the years have turned heads with this natural, sexy look—think Sophia Loren, Raquel Welch, and Farrah Fawcett. Those peek-a-boo open stitches and stretchy fabric may not make it the best choice for scuba diving, but in terms of sex appeal, it's hard to deny that the knit bikini has no match.

In this chapter, I offer patterns for both knit and crochet bikinis in several styles. Whether you like halter tops, bandeaus, barely-there tie-tops and bottoms, slinky little one-pieces, or all of the above, you'll find your favorite here. Following these patterns will save you lots of the time, frustration, and trial and error that I went through when I designed my first knit bikini, but I hope you will experiment, have fun, and make these patterns your own. I'll share the inspiration for my designs, too, but one of my goals for this book is to encourage you to be daring with your knitting: get inspired to add your own signature to a style. You can do that with color, detail, or even by substituting yarn. Escape from the cycle of predictable knits!

Each of us has our own comfort level when it comes to beachwear, so I encourage you to add or subtract rows to alter the length of any of these styles to suit your personal preferences. Part of being sexy is feeling confident, so be fearless and do what you have to do to make these styles work for you. After you put down your needles and put on your gorgeous handmade creation, get out there and have fun in the sun!

SILVER GLAM CROCHET HALTER BIKINI

STRAIGHT FROM THE CATWALK

Sizes
To fit S (M, L)

Finished Measurements
Bust to fit 32–34 (34–36, 36–38)"[81–86 (86–91.5, 91.5–96.5)cm]
Hip to fit 34–35 (36–37, 38–39)"[86–89 (91.5–94, 96.5–99)cm]

Materials
▩ 4 (5, 5) 1³⁄₄oz/50g 142yds/130m skeins of Lana Grossa Rotonda (100% Microfiber Nylon) in #2 Silver

▩ One size C/2 [2.75mm] crochet hook

▩ 1¹⁄₂yds[1.25m] of ¹⁄₄"[6mm] nylon swimwear elastic

▩ Stitch markers

Gauge
24 double crochet x 16 rows = 4 x 4"[10 x 10cm] with size C/2 crochet hook in double crochet

The glamour in this bikini comes from the silvery sheen of the nylon microfiber yarn and the finely worked stitches made with a tiny crochet hook. Don't be put off by the tiny hook—this is, after all, just a bikini. Both the halter top and bikini bottom have a decorative shell pattern. The empire line under the triangles of the bikini gives a little extra coverage and a delicate border that looks like waves. The crisscross tie on the top and the hand-braided, lace-up ties on the bottom ensure a secure, comfortable fit.

SHELL PATTERN

FOUNDATION ROW Work 1 single crochet in second chain from hook, *skip 2 chain, 5 double crochet together in next chain, skip 2 chain, 1 single crochet in next chain, repeat from * to end, turn.

ROW 1 Chain 3 (counts as double crochet), work 2 double crochet together in first single crochet, *skip 2 stitches, 1 single crochet in center of shell, skip 2 stitches, 5 double crochet together in next single crochet, repeat from *, end with 3 double crochet together in last single crochet, turn.

ROW 2 Chain 1, single crochet in first double crochet, *skip 2 stitches, 5 double crochet together in next stitch, skip 2 stitches, 1 single crochet in center of shell, repeat from *, end with 1 single crochet in top of chain 3, turn. Fasten off.

TOP

Chain 92 (104, 116). Work 8 rows of shell pattern. Work 9th row as follows: Chain 1. Work 1 single crochet in first stitch, *skip 2 stitches, work (3 double crochet, chain 3, 3 double crochet) together in next stitch, skip 2 stitches, 1 single crochet in center of shell, repeat from *, end with 1 single crochet in top of chain 3.

For Sizes Medium/Large Only Turn work upside down (shells facing down) and place marker at center. Work (90, 102), double crochet evenly across top. Decrease 3 stitches at beginning and end of next 2 (4) rows as follows: Work next 4 stitches within 1 loop of completion, yarn over hook, draw yarn through all loops—78 double crochet.

For Size Small Only Turn. Work upside down (shells facing down) and place marker at center.

From this point forward on the TOP, all sizes are worked the same

Divide for Neckline

NEXT ROW Work 39 double crochet to center. Turn.

NEXT ROW Chain 3, skip 1 double crochet, 36 double crochet, skip 1 double crochet, 1 double crochet in last double crochet—37 double crochet. Turn.

NEXT ROW Chain 3, skip 2 double crochet (at armhole), 33 double crochet, skip 1 double crochet, 1 double crochet in last double crochet—34 double crochet. Turn.

NEXT ROW Chain 3, skip 1 double crochet, double crochet to last 2 double crochet, skip 1 double crochet, 1 double crochet in last double crochet. Turn.

Repeat last row until 6 double crochet remain. At 6 double crochet, place marker and work even until piece measures 12"[30.5cm] from marker. Fasten off. Repeat for other side, reversing all shaping.

Side Tabs and Buttonholes At side, work 19 double crochet along shell rows for 6 rows.

NEXT ROW Chain 1, 1 single crochet, *skip 3 double crochet, 3 single crochet in double crochet, repeat from * 1 time, skip 3 double crochet, end with 2 single crochet (3 button-holes). Work 1 row of single crochet in each stitch. Fasten off.

FINISHING
Cut 9 strands of yarn 105"[266cm] to make one 65"[165cm] long braid with 2½"[6.5cm] long knotted ends. Crisscross through buttonholes on side tabs and tie in bow.

BOTTOM
Front Beginning at crotch seam, chain 17 (17, 19). Work 1 double crochet in 4th chain from hook, double crochet in each chain to end—14 (14, 16) double crochet.

Work 10 rows even in double crochet.

NEXT 2 ROWS Increase 1 stitch at the beginning and end of row (2 double crochet worked into 1 double crochet = 1 increase)—16 (16, 18) double crochet. Work 3 (2, 2) more rows even. Increase 1 stitch at the beginning and end of the next row—18

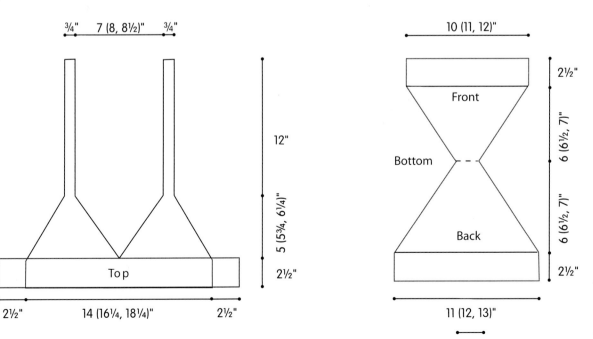

(18, 20) double crochet. Work 2 more rows even.

NEXT ROW Increase 1 stitch at the beginning and end of row. Turn.

NEXT ROW Work even. Turn. Repeat last two rows 2 more times—24 (24, 26) double crochet. Increase 1 stitch at the beginning and end of every row 0 (3, 5) times—24 (30, 36) double crochet.

NEXT ROW Increase 2 stitches at beginning and end of row—28 (34, 40) double crochet.

NEXT ROW Chain 16, turn. Work 1 double crochet in 4th chain from hook and in each of next 12 chain. Work 1 double crochet in each stitch, chain 14. Turn.

NEXT ROW Work 1 single crochet in second chain from hook (skip 2 chain, 5 double crochet together in next chain, skip 2 chain, 1 single crochet in next chain), 2 times.

Work Row 2 of shell pattern evenly across all remaining stitches—9 (10, 11) shells. Work 8 more rows of shell pattern. Fasten off.

Back Turn front section upside down and attach yarn to 14 (14, 16) double crochet at seam of crotch. Increase 1 stitch at the beginning and end of every row 2 (3, 3) times—18 (20, 22) double crochet. Increase 2 stitches at the beginning and end of every row 0 (1, 2) times—18 (24, 30) double crochet.

NEXT ROW Increase 2 stitches at the beginning and end of row.

NEXT ROW Work 1 row even.

Repeat the last two rows 10 more times—62 (68, 74) double crochet. Work row 2 of shell pattern evenly across all stitches—10 (11, 12) shells. Work 8 more rows of shell pattern. Fasten off.

FINISHING

Work 1 row of shells around all edges of front and back. Begin with 3 shells loosely worked across side edge of shell rows from waistband. Along leg openings, carry a piece of elastic like a running thread (elastic should be completely enclosed when finished).

Braided Drawstring For each, cut 9 strands of yarn 68"[173cm] to make one 40"[102cm] long braid with 2½"[6.5cm] long knotted ends. Crisscross a drawstring under 3 side shells at each side edge of waistband and tie in bow.

TINY HALTER TIE BIKINI

Sizes
To fit S (M, L)

Finished Measurements
Bust to fit 32–34 (34–36, 36–38)"[81–86 (86–91.5, 91.5–96.5)cm]
Hip to fit 34–35 (36–37,38–39)"[86–89 (91.5–94, 96.5–99)cm]

Materials
▥ 4 (6, 6) 1oz/30g 328yds/301m balls of Kaalund Yarns Enchante (100% Cultivated Silk) in Candy (MC) and 4 balls in Lavender (CC)

▥ One pair each sizes 1 [2.25mm] and 3 [3mm] knitting needles

▥ Rainbow elastic

Gauge
24 stitches x 36 rows = 4 x 4"[10 x 10cm] with size 3 needles in chevron pattern using quadruple strands

Note
All knitting is done with quadruple strands throughout.

The chevron pattern of this barely-there halter bikini is knitted in the finest 100% silk yarn, using 4 strands together and a size 3 needle. Rainbow elastic is knitted into the ribbing, offering greater stability. Braided yarn shrinks in length, so remember to cut the yarn 1½ times longer than desired for the finished length.

NOTE This bikini style is a great choice for lounging in the sun or hanging out at the beach, but because it is made with 100% silk yarn, avoid wearing it in the water.

BOTTOM

Back In MC and with size 3 needles, cast on 14 (16, 18) stitches and work 2 rows in chevron pattern (see chart on p. 26).

Sizes Medium/Large Only Increase 2 stitches in pattern at the beginning and end of every row (2, 4) times—(24, 34) stitches.

All Sizes Increase 1 stitch in pattern at the beginning and end of every row 10 (8, 7) times, every other row 16 times, every 4th row 7 (5, 3) times and every 6th row 0 (2, 3) times—80 (86, 92) stitches. Bind off.

Front Turn bottom back upside down. In MC and with size 3 needles, pick up and knit 14 (16, 18) stitches along cast-on edge. Beginning on Row 2 of chevron pattern, work 9 rows even. Increase 1 stitch at the beginning and end of every other row 0 (4, 7) times, every 4th row 14 (14, 13) times and every other row 3 (1, 2) time(s)—48 (54, 62) stitches. Bind off.

FINISHING

In CC and with size 1 needles, pick up and knit 144 (152, 160) stitches along each leg opening and work in knit 1, purl 1 rib for 3 rows, carrying rainbow elastic along purl stitches as a running thread. Bind off in rib. Also in CC and with size 1 needles, pick up and knit 48 (54, 62) stitches along the top edge for front and 80 (86, 92) stitches along the back, and work 3 rows of knit 1, purl 1 rib carrying rainbow elastic. Bind off in rib.

Ties Cut three 33-strand bunches of CC 42"[106cm] long. Thread all 99 strands halfway through the upper corner of bottom, braid and knot ends. This will make a 14"[35cm] long, ½"[1.25cm] thick braid. Repeat for the other 3 corners.

TOP

In MC and with size 3 needles, cast on 24 (30, 36) stitches. Work in chevron pattern, decreasing 1 stitch at the beginning and end of every 6th row 3 times, every 4th row 8 (7, 6) times, and every other row 0 (4, 8) times. Bind off remaining 2 stitches. Make one more cup.

FINISHING

In CC and with size 1 needles, pick up and knit 52 (56, 60) stitches along one side edge of top and work 3 rows in knit 1, purl 1 rib, carrying rainbow elastic along purl stitches. Bind off in rib. Repeat for the other side. In CC and with size 1 needles, pick up and knit 30 (36, 42) stitches along entire bottom edge of top and work 6 rows of knit 1, purl 1 rib for casing.

NEXT ROW (RS) Purl. Work in knit 1, purl 1 rib for 6 more rows and bind off in rib. Fold edge of casing along purl row and sew to wrong side of top.

Cut three 33-strand bunches of CC 2¼yds[2m] long, to make ½"[1.25cm] thick 54"[134cm] long braid. Knot ends and thread through both casings of top. Make an 18"[46cm] braid by cutting three 33-strand bunches of 54"[134cm] long yarn. Thread all 99 strands halfway through top corner of top, and tie a knot. Braid and knot ends. Repeat for other cup.

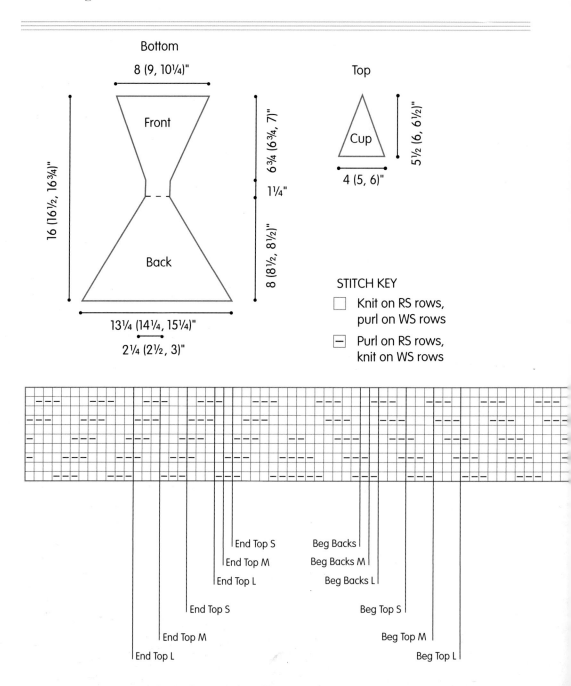

STITCH KEY
□ Knit on RS rows, purl on WS rows
− Purl on RS rows, knit on WS rows

BANDEAU BUTTERFLY CROCHET BIKINI

CAUTION: EVEN SEXIER WHEN WET

Sizes
To fit S (M, L)

Finished Measurements
Bust will stretch to fit 33 (36, 38)"[84 (91.5, 96.5)cm]
Hip will stretch to fit 34½ (37½, 40)"[87.5 (95, 101.5)cm]

Materials
▥ 4 (5, 5) 1¾ oz/50g 100yd/91m balls of Cascade Fixation (98.3% Cotton, 1.7% Elastic) in #2706 Turquoise

▥ One size C/2 [2.75mm] crochet hook

▥ 4yds[3.5m] of ¼"[6mm] nylon swimwear elastic

▥ Stitch markers

▥ Lycra lining (if desired)

Gauge
24 stitches x 17 rows = 4 x 4"[10 x 10cm] with C/2 crochet hook in double crochet

This is a bikini for social butterflies everywhere. The openwork pattern of the bandeau looks like butterflies when crocheted. The bottom is worked in single crochet, with the same open butterfly stitch along the waist. For the bandeau, the repeat is worked vertically across all stitches of the chart. For the waist of the bikini bottom, the repeat is worked horizontally, as indicated on the chart. Cascade Fixation yarn makes this a stretchy, comfortable fit that moves with you.

BOTTOM
Back Beginning at crotch seam, chain 17 (19, 19).

ROW 1 Double crochet in 4th chain from hook and double crochet in each remaining chain to end. Chain 3, turn.

ROWS 2–3 Work even in double crochet—14 (16, 16) double crochet.

ROW 4 Work 2 double crochet in first double crochet (increase 1), double crochet until 1 double crochet remains, work 2 double crochet in last double crochet (increase 1). Chain 3, turn. (2 stitches have been increased.)

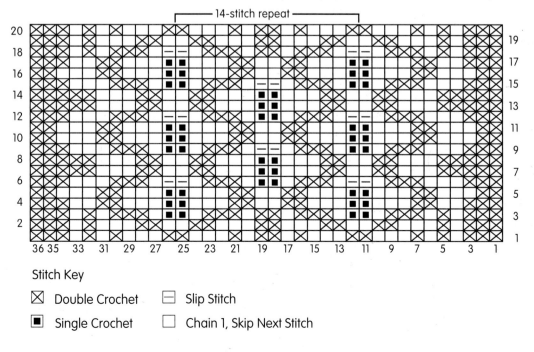

Stitch Key
⊠ Double Crochet   ⊟ Slip Stitch

■ Single Crochet   ☐ Chain 1, Skip Next Stitch

NEXT 4 (4, 5) ROWS Repeat row 4—24 (26, 28) double crochet.

NEXT 9 (10, 11) ROWS Work 3 double crochet in first double crochet (increase 2), double crochet until 1 double crochet remains, work 3 double crochet in last double crochet (increase 2). Chain 3, turn (4 stitches have been increased)—60 (60, 72) double crochet.

NEXT 2 ROWS Repeat row 4—64 (70, 76) double crochet.

NEXT ROW Work even.

NEXT ROW Repeat row 4. Repeat last 2 rows 2 times more—70 (76, 82) double crochet.

NEXT ROW Work even to end, chain 9, turn.

NEXT ROW Double crochet in 4th chain from hook and double crochet in each of next 5 chains, double crochet to end, chain 9, turn.

NEXT ROW Double crochet in 4th chain from hook and double crochet in each of next 5 chains, double crochet to end, chain 3, turn—82 (88, 94) double crochet.

NEXT ROW *Yarn over hook and pull loop through double crochet, wrap yarn around hook and draw through first 2 loops, repeat from * in next double crochet (4 loops on hook), draw yarn through all remaining loops (decrease 1), double crochet to last 2 double crochet, work decrease 1, chain 3, turn—80 (86, 92) double crochet.

NEXT ROW Work decrease 1 over next 2 double crochet 2 times, double crochet to last 4 double crochet, work decrease one 2 times, fasten off 76 (82, 88) double crochet.

Front Turn bottom back upside down and work 14 (16, 16) double crochet along crotch edge, chain 3, turn.

Work 10 rows even in double crochet.

NEXT 1 (1, 2) INCREASE ROWS Work 2 double crochet in first double crochet (increase 1), double crochet until 1 double crochet remains, work 2 double crochet in last double crochet (increase 1). Chain 3, turn. (2 stitches have been increased)—16 (18, 20) double crochet.

NEXT ROW Work even in double crochet.

NEXT ROW Repeat increase row 1. Repeat last 2 rows 2 times more—22 (24, 26) double crochet.

NEXT 5 ROWS Repeat increase row 1—32 (34, 36) double crochet.

NEXT 4 (5, 6) ROWS Work 3 double crochet in 1st double crochet (increase 2), double crochet until 1 double crochet remains, work 3 double crochet in last double crochet (increase 2). Chain 3, turn—48 (54, 60) double crochet.

NEXT ROW Repeat last row—52 (58, 64) double crochet. Chain 7, turn.

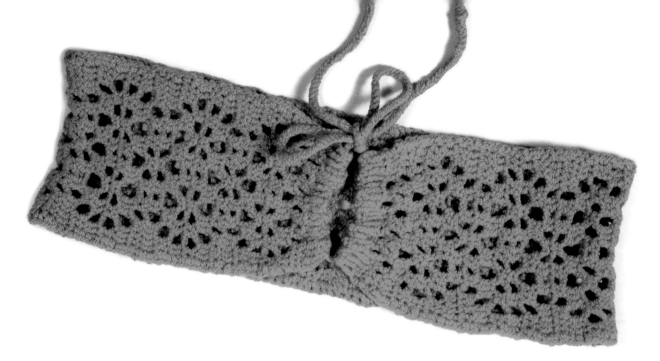

NEXT ROW Work double crochet in 4th chain from hook and each of next 3 chain, double crochet to end, chain 7, turn.

NEXT ROW Work double crochet in 4th chain from hook and each of next 3 chain, double crochet to end, chain 3, turn—60 (66, 72) double crochet.

NEXT ROW Work decrease 1, double crochet to last 2 double crochet, work decrease 1, chain 3, turn—58 (64, 70) double crochet.

NEXT ROW Work decrease 1 over next 2 double crochet 2 times, double crochet to last 4 double crochet, work decrease 1 over next 2 double crochet 2 times, fasten off 54 (60, 66) double crochet.

Do not block pieces. Sew front and back seams at waist and crotch. There are 130 (142, 154) stitches around front and back waist.

Bottom Waist With RS facing, join yarn with a slip stitch in front side of hip.

INCREASE ROW Chain 1, working around in single crochet, increase 66 (68, 70) stitches evenly spaced along top edge of front and back, join round with a slip stitch in first single crochet—196 (210, 224) single crochet.

SETUP ROW Chain 3, work row 2 of 14-stitch repeat 14 (15, 16) times, join round with a slip stitch in 3rd chain of beginning chain-3. Continue to work to row 19 of chart, beginning and ending rounds as follows: when first stitch is a double crochet, chain 3, then join round with a slip stitch in 3rd chain of beginning chain-3. When first stitch is a single crochet, chain 1, then join round with a slip stitch in beginning chain-1. When first stitch is a slip stitch, do not chain and do not join round. When first stitch is a "chain 1, skip next stitch," chain 3, then join round with a slip stitch in 3rd chain of beginning chain-3.

Knit bikinis have to be stretchy and possess some flexibility, and Cascade's yarn Fixation works perfectly for almost any bikini design. I used it for this "Bandeau Butterfly Crochet Bikini"—one of the most popular bikinis from my collection. It's a peek-a-boo style that requires sewing in a lycra lining by hand, but it's well worth the extra time.

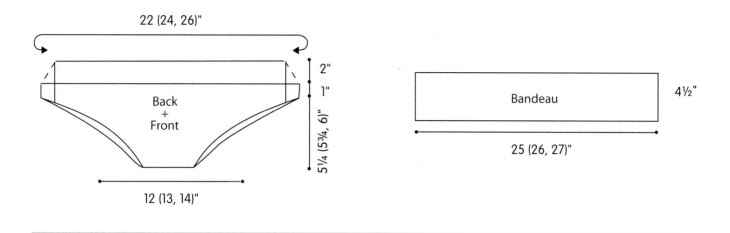

DECREASE ROUND Join elastic and work with both strands held together. Chain 1, working in single crochet, decrease 64 (70, 76) stitches evenly spaced around top front and back edges. Fasten off. Securely knot ends of elastic. Draw in ends of yarn and elastic into stitches.

Leg Opening Work 1 row of single crochet around the entire leg opening, carrying 1 piece of elastic like a running thread. Knot ends of elastic securely. Fasten off. Hide ends. Repeat as above for second leg opening.

BANDEAU

Chain 39. Beginning in 4th chain from hook, work row 1 of chart over 36 stitches. Work rows 2–13 of chart. Repeat rows 8 through 13 of chart until piece is 23 (24, 25)"[58.5 (61, 63.5)cm]. After row 13, continue in pattern, working rows 14 through 20 until piece measures 24 (25, 26)"[61 (63.5, 66)cm] or desired fit.

Single crochet a 24 (25, 26)"[61 (63.5, 66)cm] piece of elastic across top edge of bandeau. Repeat for bottom edge of bandeau.

(For more coverage, work 1 additional row of single crochet across top and bottom.) Secure elastic ends with needle and thread. Hide ends.

Neck Tie Casing

ROW 1 Begin at one corner of bandeau end, chain 4. Work 1 treble crochet, *chain 1, skip 1 stitch, work 1 treble crochet; repeat from * to end, chain 4, turn.

ROW 2 Repeat row 1. Fasten off.

Repeat rows 1 and 2 of drawstring casing at other end of bandeau.

Fold 2nd row of treble crochet casing over the first row toward WS. Sew in place.

Neck Tie Crochet a 40"[101cm] long chain. Work 1 row of slip stitch into each chain to end. Fasten off.

FINISHING

Insert each end of drawstring up through casing openings and knot ends. If desired, sew in a lycra lining by hand.

BLUE SUEDE BIKINI

DIG THIS, BO DEREK!

Sizes
To fit S (M, L)

Finished Measurements
Bust to fit 32–34 (34–36, 36–38)"[81–86 (86–91.5, 91.5–96.5)cm]
Hip to fit 34–35 (36–37, 38–39)"[86–89 (91.5–94, 96.5–99)cm]

Materials
▨ 3 (3, 4) 1³/₄oz/50g 120yds/111m balls of Berroco Suede (100% Nylon) in #3789 Nelly Belle
Water-friendly yarn substitute: 5 (5, 6) ⁷/₈ oz/25g, 85yds/78m balls of Berroco Metallic FX (85% rayon, 15% metallic)

▨ One pair size 6 [4mm] needles

▨ One size G/6 [4mm] crochet hook

▨ 1¹/₂yd[1.25m] of ¹/₄"[6mm] nylon swimwear elastic

Gauge
22 stitches x 32 rows = 4 x 4"[10 x 10cm] on size 6 needles in stockinette stitch. Gauge for substitute yarn: 22 stitches x 31 rows = 4 x 4"[10 x 10cm] on size 8 needles

This velvety soft, faux-suede bikini is knit in a simple eyelet lace pattern combined with easy-to-knit stockinette stitch. The bikini bottom has two rows of single crochet around the top edges. Elastic is worked into the leg openings and around the top edges of the waist for a snug, secure fit.

NOTE: This faux-suede bikini is great for beach parties and sun lounging, but it's not meant for wearing in the water. If you want to wear it swimming, use the substitute Berroco Metallic FX yarn in the materials list (see gauge for substitute yarn).

BOTTOM

Front Cast on 49 (55, 61) stitches. Work in lace pattern according to chart 1 for 24 rows and then continue in stockinette stitch. At the same time, decrease 2 stitches on each side every 4th row 9 (10, 11) times, and 1 stitch at the beginning and end of every 4th row 1 time—11 (13, 15) stitches. Work 24 rows even. Increase 1 stitch at the beginning and end of every other row 0 (6, 12) times and every 3rd row 16 (12, 8) times—43 (49, 55) stitches. From this point forward, work in lace pattern following chart 2. Continue increases at the beginning

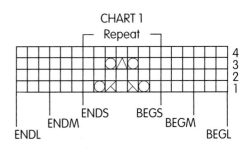

CHART 1
Repeat

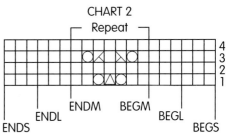

CHART 2
Repeat

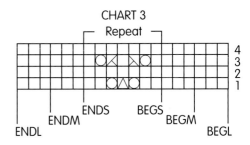

CHART 3
Repeat

Stitch Key

☐ Knit on RS rows, Purl on WS rows

◯ Yarn over

⊠ Skip 1, knit 1, pass slip stitch over

⊠ Knit 2 together

◸ Skip 1, knit 2 together, pass slip stitch over

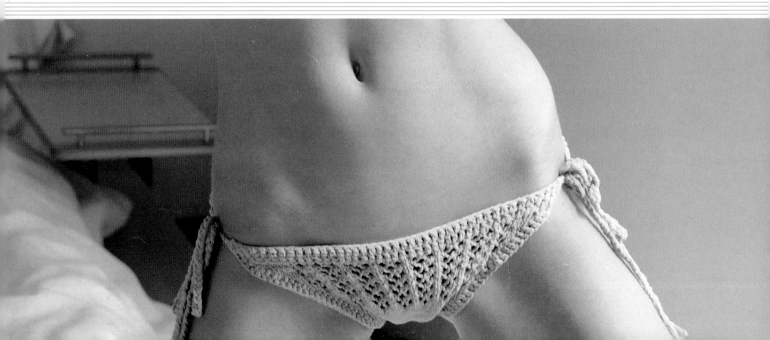

FAUX SUEDE IS SUPER SEXY

AND VERY RETRO.

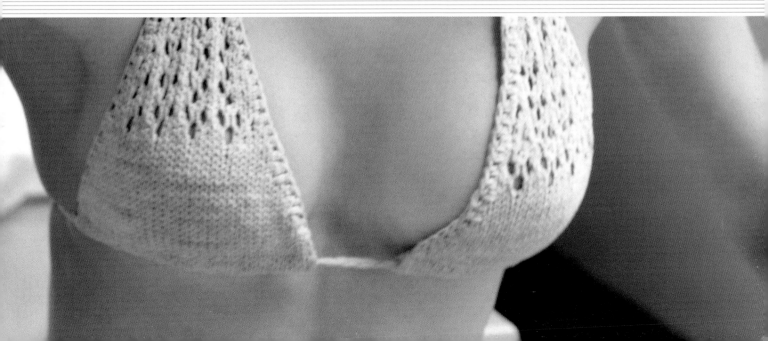

With crochet hook, work 2 rows of single crochet around the top edges of each cup only (do not work along bottom edge).

Working with the elastic (carry the yarn over the top of the elastic before you wrap the yarn over the hook to crochet), single crochet each side leg opening. Secure the ends of the elastic. Work 2 rows of double crochet across the top of the front and back bottom.

For the top, fold the bottom 5 rows of each cup to WS and sew in place. For the bottom, fold the top 5 rows of the front and back to WS and sew in place.

Braided Chains Cut 3 strands of yarn $1\frac{1}{2}$ times longer than the desired length for each braid. Make 3 even stacks until you get your desired thickness and then braid. Knot the ends. Make chains of your desired length to attach at the neckline and hips. Try on the garment to determine its length.

and end of every 3rd row for the remaining 24 rows—59 (65, 71) stitches. Bind off.

TOP

Cast on 33 (37, 39) stitches. Work even in stockinette stitch for 10 rows. Decrease 1 stitch at the beginning and end of every 3rd row 6 times for 18 rows, 21 (25, 27) stitches. Begin working the lace pattern according to chart 3 throughout. Continue decreasing 1 stitch at the beginning and end of every 3rd row until 3 stitches remain. Knit 3 together. Fasten off. Make one more cup.

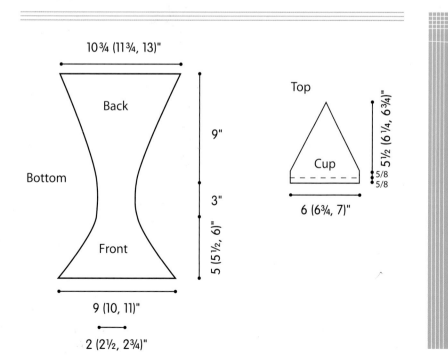

10¾ (11¾, 13)"

Back

9"

Bottom

3"

5 (5½, 6)"

9 (10, 11)"

2 (2½, 2¾)"

Front

Top

Cup

5½ (6¼, 6¾)"

5/8
5/8

6 (6¾, 7)"

You must have at least one sexy tie bikini in your summer wardrobe! The "Blue Suede Bikini" is a basic triangle-shape style with braided ties in my beloved Berroco "Suede" yarn, which is 100% nylon, although it feels as soft as real suede. This style has more coverage on the top, but a little less on the bottom—inspired by flower child, '60s style, low-riding bikinis.

MESH ONE-PIECE

Sizes

To fit S (M, L)

Finished Measurements

All finished measurements stretch to fit. Bust 34 (36, 38)"[86.5 (91.5, 96.5)cm] Hip 35½ (38½, 40)"[90 (98, 101.5)cm]

Materials

▤ 4 (5, 6) 1¾oz/50g balls of Cascade Yarns Fixation (98.3% Cotton, 1.7% Elastic) in #9674

▤ One pair size 6 [4mm] needles

▤ One size C/2 [2.75mm] crochet hook

▤ Size 4 [3.5mm] double-pointed needles

▤ Stitch holders

▤ 1½yd[1.25m] of ¼"[6mm] nylon swimwear elastic

Gauge

22 stitches x 42 rows = 4 x 4"[10 x 10cm] on size 6 needles in stockinette stitch

This surprisingly slinky one-piece is basically a bra and panty in stockinette, connected by a sexy open-work mesh bodice. The back is completely mesh, except for the bottom. The top ties for a push-up effect at the empire line, and there is an open keyhole from waist to bust. The center drawstring will slide easily through the holes to make the bust of the one-piece more fitted—just be sure to leave openings where the pattern indicates when working the final row of inner crochet around the edges of the center bust to allow for the center drawstring.

BOTTOM

Beginning at top front edge, with size 6 needles, cast on 80 (86, 92) stitches. Work in stockinette stitch for 6 (8, 10) rows. Increase 1 stitch at the beginning and end of the next row and every following 6th row 5 times more—92 (98, 104). Bind off 25 (28, 31) stitches at the beginning of the next 2 rows—42 stitches. Decrease 1 stitch at the beginning and end of every row 14 times—14 stitches. Work 32 rows even. Cast on 4 stitches at the beginning of the next 6 (8, 10) rows, increase 2 stitches at the beginning and end of every other row 0 (2, 1) time(s), increase 1 stitch at the beginning and end of every 3rd row 1 time, increase 2 stitches at the beginning and end of every 3rd row 12 (9, 10) times, increase 1 stitch at the beginning and end of every 3rd row 0 (1, 0) time, increase 1 stitch at the beginning and end of every other row 2 times—92 (98, 104) stitches. Decrease 1 stitch at the beginning and end of every 6th row 6 times—80 (86, 92) stitches. Work 6 (8, 10) rows even. Bind off.

MESH TOP BACK

Pick up 80 (86, 92) stitches evenly along bound-off edge of back bottom. Work in mesh pattern as follows:

ROW 1 (RS) Knit 1, *yarn over, knit 2 together, repeat from * to last stitch, knit 1.

ROW 2 (WS) Purl.

Repeat the last 2 rows to create the mesh pattern. At the same time, decrease 1 stitch at the beginning and end of every 8th row 5 times—70 (76, 82) stitches. Work even until the mesh section measures 7"[18cm] from the beginning.

NEXT ROW (RS) Increase 1 stitch at the beginning and end of row.

NEXT ROW (WS) Purl.

NEXT ROW (RS) Increase 1 stitch in first stitch, pattern across next 34 (37, 40) stitches, join a second ball of yarn and bind off the center 2 stitches, pattern across 34 (37, 40) stitches, increasing 1 stitch in the last stitch—36 (39, 41) stitches each half (continue working both sides of the back at the same time).

NEXT ROW (WS) Purl. Increase 1 stitch at each side edge every other row 3 times more while working center neckline even— 39 (42, 45) stitches each half.

NEXT ROW (WS) Purl.

Neckline Shaping Decrease 1 stitch at each neck edge on the next row and then every 4th row 4 times, every 5th row 1 time,

every 6th row 5 (1, 0) time(s), every 4th row 0 (5, 0) times, every 3rd row 6 (8, 17) times. At the same time, when piece measures 14 (14¼, 14½)"[35.5 (36, 37)cm] from leg opening, begin armhole shaping.

Armhole Shaping Decrease 1 stitch each armhole edge on the next row and then every 3rd row 17 times. Continue shaping the neck and armhole until 5 stitches remain. Work even on remaining stitches until armhole measures 8½ (8¾, 9¼)"[21.5 (22, 23.5)cm]. Place stitches on holders.

FRONT

Work as for the back until 3"[7.5cm] of mesh has been worked.

Divide for Center Opening Using a 2nd ball of yarn, work both sections of the front at the same time, with no shaping in center and shaping sides as for the back. Work as established until mesh section measures 7"[18cm] from the beginning.

NEXT ROW (RS) Working in stockinette stitch from this point forward, increase 5 stitches across each half of front on the next row—40 (43, 46) stitches each side. Work even until the length measures the same as for the back to armhole. Work armhole shaping as for the back. At the same time, begin decreasing 1 stitch at each neck edge every 3rd row 18 (21, 24) times until 5 stitches remain. Work until the piece measures the same length as the back and place stitches on holders.

FINISHING

Do not block pieces. Sew side and crotch seams.

I-Cords With double-pointed needle, cast on 3 stitches. *NEXT ROW (RS) With 2nd double-pointed needle, knit 4, do not turn. Slide stitches back to beginning of needle to work next row from RS; repeat from * for I-cord. Work an I-cord 42"[106.5cm] long for the bust and one 2yds[1.75m] long for cen-

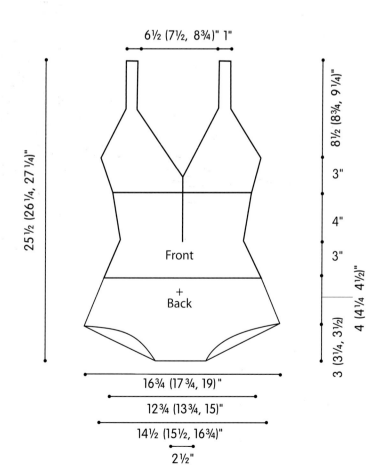

6½ (7½, 8¾)" 1"

8½ (8¾, 9¼)"

3"

4"

3"

4 (4¼, 4½)"

3 (3¼, 3½)"

Front

+
Back

25½ (26¼, 27¼)"

16¾ (17¾, 19)"

12¾ (13¾, 15)"

14½ (15½, 16¾)"

2½"

ter front. Try on mesh one-piece. Adjust length of straps, if necessary. Bind off. Sew shoulder seams. Work 1 row of single crochet around leg openings, carrying a piece of elastic, then working from left to right (without elastic), work 1 row of reverse single crochet. Fasten off. Work 1 row of single crochet around armholes, then 1 row of reverse single crochet. Fasten off. For neck edging, join yarn with a slip stitch in first stitch of first row of stockinette stitch sec-

tion of top right front. *Chain 3, skip next 3 rows; repeat from * to beginning of neck shaping for eyelets. Continue in single crochet around neck edge to beginning of left front neck shaping. Repeat from * to * for eyelets. Fasten off. With RS facing, rejoin yarn in first single crochet at beginning of left neck shaping. Work 1 row of reverse single crochet to beginning of right neck shaping. Fasten off.

HIPPIE HALTER TOP

Sizes
To fit S (M, L)

Finished Measurements
Bust to fit 34 (36, 38)"[86 (91.5, 96.5)cm]
Length 11½ (12½, 14½)"[29 (31.5, 37)cm]

Materials
▦ 3 (4, 4) ¾oz/50g 103yds/95m balls of Debbie Bliss Cotton Cashmere (85% cotton, 15% cashmere) in #150-03 Cream

▦ One size G/6 [4mm] crochet hook

▦ 1½ yds[1.5m] of ¼"[6mm] nylon swimwear elastic

Gauge
16 double crochet x 8 rows = 4 x 4"[10 x 10cm] with G/6 hook

This fringed, lattice-like hippie top gives teasing glimpses of midriff and feels soft and tickly against your skin. It combines single crochet with decorative filet crochet, which is composed of chains and doubles combined to form a lacy, net-like pattern. The top also features beautiful crochet clusters with darling fringe that gives it sway and length. The ties on the bottom and top have elongated crochet stitches, which you create by inserting a finger into a stitch to elongate it by an inch. You can alternate between regular single crochet and elongated crochet stitches, as we did, to achieve an open, chain-like effect.

HALTER
Chain 48 (54, 60).

ROW 1 Work 1 double crochet into 4th chain from hook, work 1 double crochet in each chain to end—45 (51, 57) double crochet. Turn.

ROW 2 LEFT CUP Chain 5, skip 3 stitches, 1 double crochet, chain 2, skip 2 stitches, 3 (6, 9) double crochet, *2 double crochet in next stitch, 1 double crochet, repeat from * 3 more times, 1 double crochet.

CENTER EYELETS Chain 1, skip 2 stitches, 1 double crochet, chain 1, skip 2 stitches, 2 double crochet in next stitch, chain 1, skip 2 stitches, 1 double crochet, chain 1, skip 2 stitches.

RIGHT CUP 1 double crochet, *1 double crochet, 2 double crochet in next stitch, repeat from * 3 more times, 3 (6, 9) double crochet, chain 2, skip 2 stitches, 1 double crochet, chain 2, 1 double crochet. Turn.

ROW 3 Chain 5, skip 2 stitches, 1 double crochet, chain 2, skip 2 stitches, 3 (6, 9) double crochet, *2 double crochet in next stitch, 2 double crochet, repeat from * 3 more times; chain 1, skip 1 stitch, 1 double crochet, chain 1, skip 1 stitch, 2 double crochet in next stitch, chain 1, skip 1 stitch, 1 double crochet, chain 1, skip 1 stitch; *2 double crochet, 2 double crochet in next stitch, repeat from * 3 more times, 3 (6, 9) double crochet, chain 2, skip 2 stitches, 1 double crochet, chain 2, skip 2 stitches, 1 double crochet. Turn.

ROW 4 Chain 5, skip 2 stitches, 1 double crochet, chain 1, skip 2 stitches, 6 (9, 12) double crochet, make 1 double-crochet

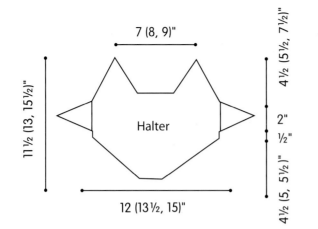

7 (8, 9)"

11½ (13, 15½)"

Halter

4½ (5½, 7½)"

2"

½"

4½ (5, 5½)"

12 (13½, 15)"

cluster decrease [work 1 double crochet into each of next 2 stitches leaving last loop of each on hook. Yarn over and draw through all loops on hook], 9 double crochet; chain 1, skip 1 stitch, 1 double crochet, chain 1, skip 1 stitch, 2 double crochet in next stitch, chain 1, skip 1 stitch, 1 double crochet, chain 1, skip 1 stitch; 9 double crochet, make 1 double-crochet cluster decrease, 6 (9, 12) double crochet, chain 1, skip 2 stitches, 1 double crochet, chain 1, skip 2 stitches, 1 double crochet. Turn.

ROW 5 Chain 4, skip 1 stitch, 1 double crochet into double crochet, skip 1 stitch, 16 (19, 22) double crochet; chain 1, skip 1 stitch, 1 double crochet, chain1, skip 1 stitch, 2 double crochet in next stitch, chain 1, skip 1 stitch, 1 double crochet, chain 1, skip 1 stitch; 16 (19, 22) double crochet, skip 1 stitch, 1 double crochet into double crochet, skip 1 stitch, 1 double crochet. Turn.

ROW 6 Chain 3 (double crochet 3 counts as 1 double crochet), skip 1 stitch, 1 double crochet into double crochet, skip 1 stitch, 16 (19, 22) double crochet; chain 1, skip 1 stitch, 1 double crochet, chain 1, skip 1 stitch, 2 double crochet in next stitch, chain 1, skip 1 stitch, 1 double crochet, chain 1, skip 1 stitch; 16 (19, 22) double crochet, skip 1 stitch, 1 double crochet into double crochet, skip 1 stitch, 1 double crochet. Turn.

For size Medium, repeat row 6 once more. For size Large, repeat row 6 twice more. For size Small, continue to row 7.

ROW 7 Chain 3, 16 (19, 22) double crochet, skip 1 stitch, 1 double crochet in double crochet, chain 4, 1 single crochet in middle of 2 double crochet, chain 4, skip 1 stitch, 1 double crochet into next double crochet, 17 (20, 23) double crochet. Turn. Work one side of cup until finished.

ROW 8 Chain 3, make 1 double-crochet cluster decrease, 12 (15, 18) double crochet, make 1 double-crochet cluster decrease, 1 double crochet. Turn.

ROW 9 Chain 3, make 1 double-crochet cluster decrease, 10 (13, 16) double crochet, make 1 double-crochet cluster decrease, 1 double crochet. Turn.

ROW 10 Chain 3, make 1 double-crochet cluster decrease, 8 (11, 14) double crochet, make 1 double-crochet cluster decrease, 1 double crochet. Turn.

ROW 11 Chain 3, make 1 double-crochet cluster decrease 2 times (over next 4 double crochet), 2 (5, 8) double crochet, make 1 double-crochet cluster decrease 2 times, 1 double crochet. Turn.

ROW 12 Chain 3, make 1 double-crochet cluster decrease 4 (5, 7) times to end. Turn.

For sizes Small and Medium, continue to row 13. For Large, work row 12A (see below) and continue to row 13.

ROW 12A (FOR LARGE ONLY) Chain 3, make 1 double-crochet cluster decrease 4 times. Turn.

ROW 13 Chain 3, 5 double-crochet cluster decrease (work a 1 double crochet into each remaining double crochet, leaving the last loop of each on hook; yarn over hook and draw through all loops on hook).

Begin at row 8, work second cup same as the first.

Lattice Bottom Begin at right bottom edge of top chain 5 in 1 stitch double crochet, skip 3 double crochet, 1 double crochet between 3rd and 4th double crochet, *chain 2, skip 3 stitches, 1 double crochet between 3rd and 4th skipped double crochet, to end 15 (17, 19) loops.

Although I do not use leather or fur in any of my designs, I am often inspired by the earth tones, silhouettes, and funky craftsmanship of '70s vintage leather pieces, many of which were handcrafted. To give this halter faux-suede funkiness, use the Berroco Suede yarn recommended for the "Tie Bottom" on page 50—wear the halter and bottom together to really turn some heads. Add beads or shells to the ties of the halter for weight and a fun chime effect.

MAKES A DARLING SUMMER HALTER

NEXT ROW Chain 3, 1 double crochet in double crochet of previous row, *chain 2, skip 2 stitches, 1 double crochet in double crochet of previous row, repeat from * until 1 double crochet remains, 1 double crochet. Repeat last row until 2 full and 2 half-side loops remain across the bottom, approximately 9 (10, 11) rows.

Side Triangle Tab (Make 2) Begin at the bottom side of top (between first full row of double crochet and first lattice mesh of bra). Chain 3 (counts as 1 double crochet), work 3 double crochet in 1 mesh of bra 3 (4, 4) times—10 (13, 13) stitches. Work 4 (5, 5) rows decreasing 2 double crochet per row (working in between double crochet of row below will decrease number of stitches).

LAST ROW Chain 3, work 1 double crochet in between any remaining stitches within 1 loop of completion, yarn over hook and draw through all loops. Fasten off.

Ties Cut three 54"[137cm] long strands of yarn. String halfway through top of cup.

FOR HOT, SULTRY DAYS.

With all six strands and crochet hook, *chain 1 then elongate by inserting finger into chain to lengthen the stitch; repeat from * to end. Chain should measure approximately 18"[46cm] long. Knot end. Repeat for other cup and each side triangle tab.

Fringe Cut three 12"[30.5cm] long strands of yarn for each fringe. Referring to photo, knot fringe along bottom front edge of halter.

Lacing Crochet a chain to measure 24"[61cm]. Fasten off. Lace up center front through eyelets between cups.

TIE BOTTOM

Sizes
To fit S (M, L)

Finished Measurements
Hip to fit 34–35 (36–37, 38–39)"[86–89 (91.5–94, 96.5–99)cm]

Length 16 (17, 18)"[40.5 (43, 46)cm]

Materials
▥ 1 (2, 2) 1³⁄₄oz/50g 120yds/111m balls of Berroco Suede (100% Nylon) in #3754 Annie Oakley

▥ One size E/4 [3.5mm] crochet hook

▥ 1 yd[1m] of ¹⁄₄"[6mm] nylon swimwear elastic

Gauge
20 double crochet x 10 rows = 4 x 4"[10 x 10cm] with E/4 hook

Make this tiny, sexy tie bottom in many different colors to go with your favorite halter, T-shirt, or camisole. Its rows of decorative single crochet and filet stitch match beautifully with the Hippie Halter (see page 44).

BOTTOM

Front Chain 33 (37, 43).

ROW 1 Work 1 double crochet in 4th chain from hook, 1 double crochet in each chain to end—30 (34, 40) double crochet. Chain 3, turn.

ROWS 2 TO 12 (14, 16) *Yarn over hook and pull loop through double crochet, wrap yarn around hook and draw through first 2 loops, repeat from * in next double crochet (4 loops on hook), draw yarn through all remaining loops (decease 1 double crochet), double crochet to last 2 double crochet, work decrease 1 double crochet. Chain 3, turn.

Crotch Work 7 rows even in double crochet.

Back

NEXT ROW Work 2 double crochet (increase) at the beginning and end of row.

NEXT ROW Work even.

Repeat last 2 rows 9 times more—48 (48, 50) stitches. Increase 1 double crochet at beginning and end of every row 3 (5, 7) times—54 (58, 64) stitches.

Lattice Top

ROW 1 Chain 3, 1 double crochet in next double crochet, *chain 2, skip 2 double crochet, 1 double crochet in next 3 double crochet, repeat from *, end with 1 double crochet. Turn.

Repeat row 1, once more working 1 double crochet in each double crochet.

Repeat lattice top for front.

Work 1 row of single crochet, carrying elastic as a running thread around both leg openings and across top of front and back panty.

Ties Cut three 54"[137cm] long pieces of yarn. String halfway through top corner of bottom panty. With all six strands held together and crochet hook, *chain 6, elongate next 2 chains (insert finger into chain to lengthen stitch) until desired length, repeat from * to end (approximately 18"[46cm]). Knot end. Repeat for 3 remaining sides.

CHAPTER 2

SUNSHINE, GOOD VIBES

Whether you're at a swank resort in St. Tropez or hanging out on the boardwalk at Venice Beach, you need something chic and sexy to wear when you're not in the water, and that is what this chapter is all about. Knit apparel has made a major comeback in the fashion world in the past few years, and the vintage look has inspired collections from some of the biggest knitwear labels, including the Italian company Missoni and the American luxury brand St. John. But the truth is that the hand-knitters of yesterday and today are the true pioneers of this reemerging trend—I consider them fellow designers and artists. To us, knitting clothing will never be old-fashioned.

For the designs in this chapter, I was inspired by three things: a desire to offer knitters hip, fun, summery items to make; the funky, free fashions of Woodstock; and '70s-style minidresses, jumpers, and short-shorts. Living in L.A., I am lucky because the seasons are not extreme and I can enjoy my summer knits year-round. But while lots of the knitting books out there are full of patterns for mostly fall and winter pieces, you can be sure that this chapter offers what you might have trouble finding: patterns for chic, warm-weather clothes. In fact, you should have a wardrobe full of sexy little knits that let you flaunt some bare skin no matter where you live or what season it is. Use the summer designs in this chapter as a base; make them appropriate for colder months by adding length, filling in stitches for more coverage, and substituting cotton or hemp yarn with wool or mohair of the same gauge. And remember that knitting in a different palette is one of the easiest ways to adapt any design to another season.

You are probably a fashion designer at heart or you wouldn't be reading this book, so go ahead—add your own touch to these patterns. Change the colors, experiment with stitching, add embellishment, try new yarns, try different lengths. Venture off the beaten path a little, and if it feels good—wear it!

HEMP V-NECK TOP

Sizes
To fit XS (S, M, L)

Finished Measurements
Bust 32 (35, 37, 39)"[81.5 (89, 94, 99)cm]
Waist 27 (30½, 32½, 34½)"[68.5 (77.5, 82.5, 87.5)cm]
Length 21½ (21½, 22½, 22½)"[54.5 (54.5, 57, 57)cm]

Materials
▨ 6 (8, 8, 10) 1¾oz/50g 322yds/295m balls of Hemp for Knitting Hempton (50% hemp, 50% cotton) in #101, Chocolate (MC), and 1 in #201 Natural (CC)

▨ One pair size 6 [4mm] needles

▨ One size C/2 [2.75mm] crochet hook

Gauge
23 stitches x 34 rows = 4 x 4"[10 x 10cm] with size 6 needles in stockinette stitch

Note
Yarn is doubled throughout. This includes checking gauge and all finishing.

You'll need to work with two strands of this beautiful and durable hemp yarn. It's a simple stockinette to the waist, and a gorgeous cluster-crochet shell pattern worked at the top of the front and back. You can try different looks with the sleeves. Make the crochet loops as indicated, or add a simple tack with needle and thread if you would like to take out any fullness.

SHELL CROCHET PATTERN
ROW 1 (RS) Chain 1, single crochet in first stitch, *skip 2 stitches, 5 double crochet in next stitch, skip 2 stitches, single crochet in next stitch, repeat from * to end. Turn.

ROW 2 Chain 3, 3 double crochet in first single crochet, *skip 2 stitches, 5 double crochet in next stitch, skip 2 stitches, single crochet in next stitch, repeat from *, end with 3 double crochet in last single crochet. Turn. Repeat rows 1 and 2 for pattern.

BACK
In MC, cast on 96 (106, 112, 118) stitches. Working in stockinette stitch, decrease 1 stitch at the beginning and end of every 5th row 9 (9, 5, 5) times and every 6th row 0 (0, 4, 4) times—78 (88, 94, 100) stitches.

Work even until the piece measures 6 (6, 6½, 6½)"[15 (15, 16.5, 16.5)cm] from the beginning, end on WS. Bind off all stitches loosely, leaving last loop on needle. Transfer loop to crochet hook, chain 1, turn to WS. Work 61 (73, 79, 85) single crochet evenly spaced across bound-off stitches. Turn. Work row 1 of shell pattern—10 (12, 13, 14) shells. Continue in shell pattern for 10 more rows, end on RS. Turn.

NEXT (INCREASE) ROW (WS) Chain 3, 6 double crochet in first single crochet, *skip 2 stitches, 5 double crochet in next stitch, skip 2 stitches, single crochet in next stitch, repeat from *, end with 6 double crochet in last single crochet. Turn. Work rows 2 and 1 of shell pattern—11 (13, 14, 15) shells. Turn. Repeat last 3 rows twice more—13 (15, 16, 17) shells. Work even until the piece measures 13½ (13½, 14½, 14½)"[34.5 (34.5, 37, 37)cm] from the beginning. Turn.

Armhole Shaping Slip stitch across first 3 stitches at the beginning and end of every other row 2 times—11 (13, 14, 15) shells. Work even in pattern until the armhole measures 8"[20.5cm] from the beginning. Fasten off.

FRONT
Work as for the back until the piece meas-

ures 14¼ (14¼, 15¼, 15¼)"[36 (36, 39, 39)cm] from the beginning, work neckline shaping as follows: Decrease 1 stitch, in pattern, from each side of the center neck every other row for 20 rows—2½ (3½, 4, 4½) shells at the shoulder. Work even until the piece is the same length as the back. Fasten off.

FINISHING

Block the pieces. Sew the front and back together at the shoulders.

SLEEVE CAP

ROW 1 Join CC with a slip stitch in underarm edge, single crochet in first stitch, chain 6, skip 1 shell, 1 single crochet, repeat until you have 20 loops around armhole. Turn.

ROW 2 Skip 1 loop, *chain 6, 1 single crochet in the middle of the loop, repeat from *, skip last loop to make 18 loops. Turn.

ROW 3 Skip 2 loops, *chain 6, 1 single crochet in the middle of the loop, repeat from *, skip the last 2 loops to make 14 loops. Turn.

ROWS 4, 5, 6, 7, 8 Work as row 2, skipping the first and last loop. End with 4 loops at the end of row 8. Fasten off. Sew the side seams.

In CC (working from left to right), work 1 row of reverse single crochet around the neckline and around the bottom of the sweater. Crochet a 55 (55, 60, 60)"[140 (140, 152, 152)cm] long chain as follows: work 7 normal chain stitches followed by 2 elongated chains (stick tip of finger into chain), repeat from * across, fasten off. Weave the chain drawstring through the first row of shell stitch, above stockinette stitch. Knot the ends.

Woodstock was a huge inspiration for the designs in this chapter, and what could be more Woodstock than hemp? This V-neck top is made with Hemp for Knitting in fine finger weight. The top has a cute little crochet cap sleeve and a dainty waist drawstring in a contrast color. Feel free to make it as short or long as you desire. Just be sure to plan ahead so you can adjust the length of the stockinette waist before starting the crochet top.

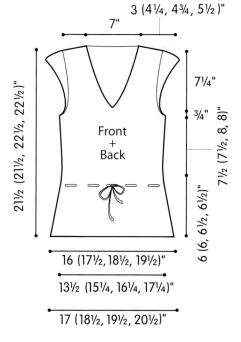

3 (4¼, 4¾, 5½)"

7"

7¼"

¾"

7½ (7½, 8, 8)"

21½ (21½, 22½, 22½)"

Front + Back

6 (6, 6½, 6½)"

16 (17½, 18½, 19½)"

13½ (15¼, 16¼, 17¼)"

17 (18½, 19½, 20½)"

DRAWSTRING COVER

WEAR THIS OVER YOUR TEENY BIKINI

Sizes
To fit S (M, L)

Finished Measurements
Bust 41 (45, 49)"[104 (114.5, 124.5)cm]
Length 24 (26, 28)"[61 (66, 71)cm]
Upper arm 17½ (18½, 19½)"[44.5 (47, 49.5)cm]

Materials
▦ 4 (5, 6) 1¾oz/50g 120 yds/111m balls of Berroco Suede (100% Nylon) in #3737 Roy Rogers

▦ One pair each of size 8 [5mm] and size 17 [12.75mm] needles

▦ One size G/6 [4mm] crochet hook

▦ Stitch holder

Gauge
8 stitches x 8 rows = 4 x 4"[10 x 10cm] on size 17 needles over lace pattern

This top knits quickly on size 17 needles. The all-over lace pattern looks difficult, but it is actually simple to knit. Extra stitches have been added to the ribbing at the cuffs and waist for a better fit, but you will work on fewer stitches for the rest of the top. It creates a beautiful silhouette. This is a perfect hot-weather top because it's got great drape and texture, but it's still cool and lets your skin breathe.

LACE PATTERN (ODD STITCHES FOR REPEAT)

ROW 1 Knit 1, *yarn over, knit 2 together, repeat from * to end. Repeat row 1 for lace pattern.

BACK

With smaller needles, cast on 71 (81, 91) stitches. Work in stockinette stitch for 1"[2.5cm], ending with a RS row.

NEXT ROW (WS) Decrease 30 (36, 42) stitches evenly across—41 (45, 49) stitches.

Change to larger needles, and work in lace pattern until the piece measures 17 (18, 19)"[43 (45.5, 48)cm] from the beginning, ending with a WS row.

Armhole Shaping Bind off 4 stitches at the beginning of the next 2 rows—33 (37, 41) stitches. Work in pattern until the armhole measures 7½ (8½, 9½)"[19 (21.5, 24)cm]. Bind off.

Front Work as for the back until the armhole measures 6½ (7½, 8½)"[16.5 (19, 21.5)cm].

Neckline Shaping

NEXT ROW (RS) Work 4 (5, 6) stitches in pattern, turn.

NEXT ROW (WS) Decrease 1 stitch, pattern to the end.

Bind off remaining 3 (4, 5) stitches.

NEXT ROW (RS) Bind off center 25 (27, 29) stitches, work 4 (5, 6) stitches to the end.

NEXT ROW (WS) Work 2 (3, 4) stitches in pattern, decrease 1.

Bind off remaining 3 (4, 5) stitches.

SLEEVES

With smaller needles, cast on 37 (40, 43) stitches. Work 1"[2.5cm] in stockinette stitch, ending with a RS row.

NEXT ROW (WS) Decrease 6 (7, 8) stitches evenly across—31 (33, 35) stitches.

NEXT ROW (RS) Change to larger needles and work 16 rows in lace pattern. Increase 1 stitch at the beginning and end of the next row—to keep in pattern begin and end rows with knit 2. Work 16 rows in pattern. Increase 1 stitch at the beginning and end of the next row—to keep in pattern begin row with knit 1 and end with knit 2 together—35 (37, 39) stitches. Work even in pattern until piece measures 18"[46cm] from the beginning. Bind off 4 stitches at the beginning of the next 2 rows. Decrease 1 stitch at the beginning and end of every 4th row 3 times—21 (23, 25) stitches. Work 0 (1, 2) row(s) even. Bind off.

FINISHING

Lightly block pieces. Sew the front and back together at shoulders. Sew the sleeves to armholes. Sew side and sleeve seams. Fold sleeve casings in half to WS and sew in place, leaving opening for drawstrings. Fold waist casing in half to WS and sew in place, leaving opening on one side for the drawstring.

Drawstrings With the crochet hook, make two 28"[71cm] long chains for the sleeve casings.

Make one 50"[127cm] long chain for the waist casing. Thread drawstrings through casings. Knot ends of drawstrings.

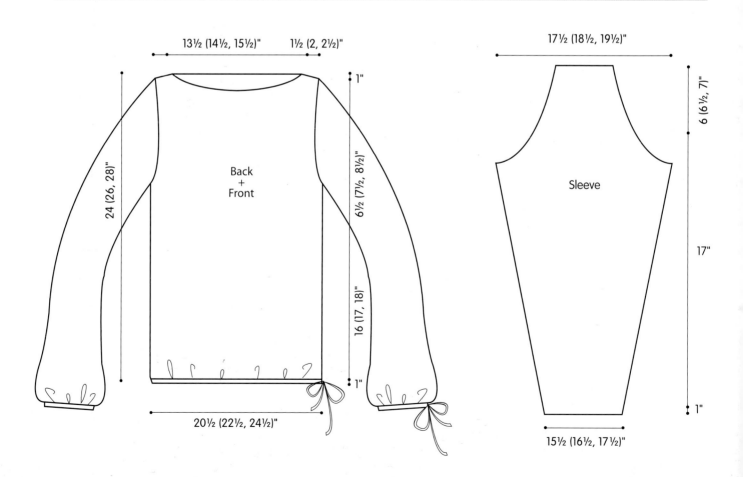

LITTLE MERMAID STRAPLESS TOP

CUSTOMIZE IT: KNIT IT SHORT OR LONG

Sizes
To fit XS (S, M, L)

Finished Measurements
All finished measurements stretch to fit
Bust 32 (34, 36, 40)"[81 (86.5, 91.5, 101.5)cm]
Hip 34 (35½, 38½, 42)"[86.5 (90, 98, 106.5)cm]

Materials
▧ 4 (5, 5, 6) 1¾oz/50g 100yds/91m balls of Cascade Fixation (98.3% Cotton, 1.7% Elastic) in #9946 (MC)

▧ 1 ball in #1198 (CC)

▧ One pair size 6 [4mm] and 7 [4.5mm] needles

▧ One size 8 [5mm] 24"[60cm] circular needle

▧ Size 7 [4.5 mm] double-pointed needles

▧ Rainbow elastic

Gauge
26 stitches x 44 rows = 4 x 4"[10 x10cm] on size 7 needles in stockinette stitch

All stockinette with additional increases that gather at the bust for a roomier fit. It has a lacey crochet ruffle at the bottom. This pattern can easily go from top to dress by making it as long as you want! Try on the garment and knit to desired length before making final bust increases. You'll need to buy extra yarn if you decide to make the design your own.

KNIT 1, PURL 1 RIB

ROW 1 *Knit 1, purl 1, repeat from * to end.

ROW 2 Knit the knit stitches and purl the purl stitches. Repeat row 2.

M1 Make 1 stitch by knitting into back loop of horizontal bar lying before next stitch.

BACK
With size 6 needles, cast on 84 (92, 100, 110) stitches in A. Work 6 rows of knit 1, purl 1 rib with elastic carried across the purl stitches. Change to size 7 needles, and work in stockinette stitch until the piece measures 3½ (3½, 3¾, 4)"[9 (9, 9.5, 10)cm] from beginning. Decrease 1 stitch at the beginning and end of every 4th row 15 times—54 (62, 70, 80) stitches. Work even until the piece measures 9½ (9¾, 10, 10¼)"[24 (25, 25.5, 26)cm] from the beginning. Increase as follows: Knit 2, M1, knit to last 2 stitches, M1, knit 2. Work increase row every 6th row 0 (0, 3, 4) times and every 8th row 9 (10, 8, 7) times—72 (82, 92, 102) stitches. Work even until the piece measures 16¾ (17, 17½, 18)"[42.5 (43, 44.5, 45.5)cm] from the beginning, ending with a RS row.

NEXT ROW (WS) Decrease 6 stitches evenly across—66 (76, 86, 96) stitches. Change to size 6 needles and work 6 rows of knit 1, purl 1 rib, carrying elastic across purl stitches. Bind off loosely in rib.

FRONT
Work as for the back until the piece measures 9½ (9¾, 10, 10¼)"[24 (25, 25.5, 26)cm] from the beginning. Increase 1 stitch at the beginning and end of every 4th row 1 (2, 3, 4) times, and every 6th row 5 times—66 (76, 86, 98) stitches. Place marker at the beginning and end of the next row. Increase 1 stitch at the beginning and end of every other row 5 (6, 6, 6) times—76 (88, 98, 110) stitches. At the same time, when piece measures 13 (13½, 14, 14¼)"[33 (34, 35.5, 36)cm] from the beginning, ending with a WS row, work the eyelet row.

Eyelet Row (worked on center 8 stitches)

NEXT ROW 1 (RS) Knit to center 8 stitches, knit 2 together, yarn over, knit 4, yarn over, knit 2 together, knit to end.

Repeat eyelet row 9 times more on every following 6th row. Continue until the piece measures 17¾ (18, 18½, 19)"[45 (45.5, 47, 48)cm] from the beginning, ending with a RS row.

NEXT ROW (WS) Decrease 8 stitches evenly across row—68 (80, 90, 102) stitches. Change to size 6 needles and work 6 rows of knit 1, purl 1 rib, carrying elastic across purl stitches. Bind off loosely.

FINISHING

Sew the side seams, starting from the bottom up to the markers. Top front gathers above markers to meet top back, stitch in place.

Ruffle Begin at the side seam.

With CC and circular needle, pick up and knit every other stitch along the front and the back bottom edges of top. Join to work in the round.

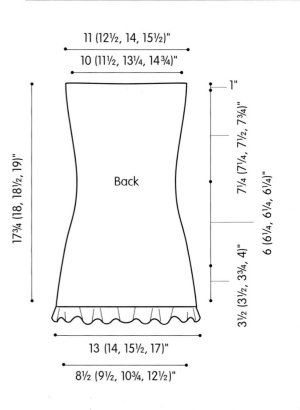

11 (12½, 14, 15½)"
10 (11½, 13¼, 14¾)"

1"

7¼ (7¼, 7½, 7¾)"

Back

6 (6¼, 6¼, 6¼)"

17¾ (18, 18½, 19)"

3½ (3½, 3¾, 4)"

13 (14, 15½, 17)"

8½ (9½, 10¾, 12½)"

NEXT ROUND Increase by knitting into the front and the back of each stitch around. Knit 1 round.

NEXT ROUND *Knit 2 together, yarn over, repeat from * until the end. Repeat the last round until the ruffle measures 2"[5cm]. Knit 1 round.

NEXT ROUND *Knit 1, yarn over, repeat from * until the end. Bind off.

Lacing With double-pointed needles and MC, cast on 3 stitches. Work 3 stitch I-cord as follows:

ROW 1 (RS) Knit to the end, slide the stitches to the opposite end of the needle for the next row.

Repeat row 1 until the piece measures 34"[86cm] from the beginning. Bind off.

Lace the I-cord through the eyelets of the front.

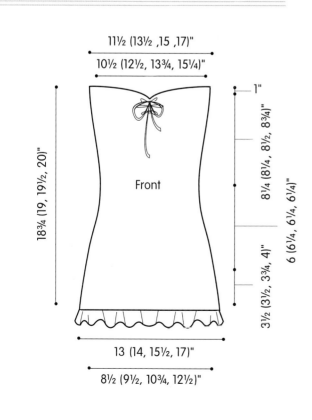

11½ (13½ ,15 ,17)"

10½ (12½, 13¾, 15¼)"

1"

8¼ (8¼, 8½, 8¾)"

6 (6¼, 6¼, 6¼)"

18¾ (19, 19½, 20)"

Front

3½ (3½, 3¾, 4)"

13 (14, 15½, 17)"

8½ (9½, 10¾, 12½)"

TERRY SHORT-SHORTS

WE WEAR SHORT-SHORTS

Sizes
To fit S (M, L)

Finished Measurements
Hip 38 (42½, 47)"[96.5 (108, 119.5)cm]
Length 8½ (9, 9¾)"[21.5 (23, 25)cm]

Materials
▨ 2 (2, 3) balls 1¾oz/ 50g 175yd/160m balls of Lana Grossa Leggero (100% Microfiber) in #42 Blue (MC) and 1 ball in #52 Yellow (CC)

▨ One pair size 8 [5mm] needles

▨ One size I/9 [5.5mm] crochet hook

▨ 1 yd[1m] of ¾"[2cm] wide elastic

▨ Stitch markers

Gauge
16 stitches x 30 rows = 4 x 4"[10 x 10cm] with size 8 needles over stockinette stitch

The low-rise elasticized waist of these brazen little short-shorts must be sewn securely with a needle or by machine. Drawstring casings are attached from the inside with crochet seams in a contrasting color, creating cute stripes at the side seams. The shorts are fuller and longer in the back than they are in the front for a comfy fit. If the low-rise is a little too low or the shorts are a little too short, feel free to customize!

BACK

Right Leg With MC, cast on 27 (29, 33) stitches.

Work 2 rows in stockinette stitch.

NEXT ROW Cast on 10 stitches at the beginning of the row at the right side seam edge. Work in stockinette stitch across this row and the following WS row.

NEXT ROW Cast on 4 stitches. Work 2 rows in stockinette stitch.

NEXT ROW (RS) Cast on 4 (6, 6) stitches. At the same time, increase for the inner leg as follows:

Increase 1 stitch at the end of every 7th (7th, 9th) row 1 time. Continue even until piece measures 2 (2¼, 2½)"[5 (6, 6.5)cm] from the beginning, ending with a RS row.

SHAPE CROTCH

NEXT ROW (WS) Bind off 6 (8, 8) stitches. Decrease 1 stitch at crotch edge on next 6 rows—34 (36, 40) stitches, purl to the end.

Decrease 1 stitch at the beginning of the next row (WS) 1 time, every other row 1 (1, 2) time(s), every 4th row 3 (2, 3) times and every 6th row 0 (1, 1) time(s)—29 (31, 33) stitches. Continue even until the piece measures 7 (7¼, 8)"[18 (18.5, 20)cm] from the beginning, place marker at the beginning of the WS row.

Work 6 rows even.

NEXT ROW (RS) Purl (casing ridge). Work 6 rows of stockinette stitch. Bind off.

Left Leg Work as for the right leg, reversing all shapings.

FRONT

Left Leg With MC, cast on 39 (42, 47) stitches. Working in stockinette stitch, increase 1 stitch at the beginning of every 7th (7th, 9th) row once. Continue even until

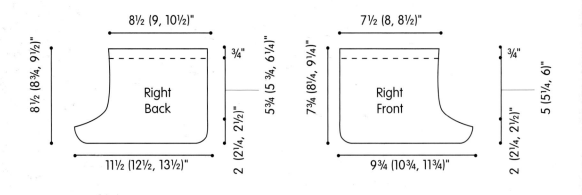

Right Back

8½ (9, 10½)"

8½ (8¾, 9½)"

¾"

5¾ (5¾, 6¼)"

2 (2¼, 2½)"

11½ (12½, 13½)"

Right Front

7½ (8, 8½)"

7¾ (8¼, 9¼)"

¾"

5 (5¼, 6)"

2 (2¼, 2½)"

9¾ (10¾, 11¾)"

the piece measures 2 (2¼, 2½)"[5 (6, 6.5)cm] from the beginning.

SHAPE CROTCH

NEXT ROW (RS) Bind off 4 stitches, knit to the end. Decrease 1 stitch at crotch edge on next 3 (3, 5) rows—33 (36, 39) stitches.

Decrease 1 stitch at the beginning of every other row 2 times and every 4th row 1 (2, 3) times—30 (32, 34) stitches. Work even until the piece measures 6¼ (6½, 7¼)"[16 (16.5, 18.5)cm] from the beginning, place marker at the end of the row.

Work 6 rows even.

NEXT ROW (RS) Purl (folding line). Work 6 rows even, bind off.

Right Leg Work as for the front left leg, reversing all shapings.

Inner Leg Casings With MC, cast on 7 stitches. Work in stockinette stitch until piece measures 7 (7¼, 8)"[18 (18.5, 20)cm] from the beginning, bind off.

FINISHING

Block the pieces without steam.

Attach Casings Sew each front and back piece together at the side seam. Center the leg casing over the wrong side of the side seam and pin in place. Bottom edge of the casing should be even with the bottom edge of the shorts and meet the purl row of casing. Using crochet hook and CC, from RS work 3 crochet seams through all thicknesses, one on each side of the casing and one seam down center. This will leave openings at the top and bottom of the casing for the drawstring.

Drawstrings (Make 2) With crochet hook and CC, work 30 (32, 34)"[76 (81, 86.5)cm] of chain stitch.

NEXT ROW Work 1 slip stitch in each chain across. Fasten off. Insert each end of drawstring into casing openings. Sew inner leg seams of the front and back together. Using back stitch, sew center front and back seam. Fold waist to inside of the shorts at purl row and sew along bottom edge of waist casing, leaving a small opening to insert elastic. Cut 27 (28, 29)"[68.5 (71, 73.5)cm] piece of elastic and insert into casting. Sew ends of elastic. Sew opening in casing.

Short-shorts are so '70s, but with a little twist, this style becomes modern and sporty. These "Terry Short-Shorts" in a Lana Grossa yarn will make the sweetest rollerblade outfit ever. Everyone will want to know where you got those shorts: don't tell!

Try making them with stripes or a contrast color banding. Get creative and make an assortment of short-shorts for the long, lazy summer.

RACING-STRIPE TERRY JUMPER

Sizes
To fit S (M, L)

Finished Measurements
Bust 32 (36, 40)"[81 (91.5,101.5)cm]
Length 26 (27, 28)"[66 (68.5, 71)cm]
Hip 34 (38, 42)"[86.5 (96.5, 106.5)cm]

Materials
▥ 8 (10, 11) 1³⁄₄oz/50g 114yds/105m balls of Wendy Velvet Touch (100% Nylon Polymide) in #1216 Baby Blue (MC) and 2 (2, 3) balls in #1209 Baby Pink (CC)

▥ Two pair size 8 [5mm] knitting needles

▥ 1 yd[91.5cm] of ¹⁄₂"[14mm]

▥ Stitch markers

▥ Stitch holders

▥ Yarn needle

▥ Sewing needle and thread (optional—use if sewing elastic ends by hand)

Gauge
16 stitches x 28 rows = 4 x 4"[10 x 10cm] with size 8 needles over stockinette stitch

What's sportier and cuter than a baby-blue strapless terry jumper? This garment is wider across the top front and back bottom for additional ease and room. All of this extra fullness is increased and decreased at the waist. Straight side seams give a cleaner look that blouses gracefully over the waistline. I recommend securing the ends of the bust and waist elastic with a sewing machine, but you can also do this by hand with needle and thread.

BACK

Right Bottom With MC, cast on 35 (39, 42) stitches. In stockinette stitch, work side seam shaping (beginning of RS rows and end of WS rows) as follows: increase 1 stitch on every row 2 times, every other row 2 (1, 1) time(s), every 4th row 1 (1, 2) time(s) and every 6th row 2 (3, 3) times, at the same time, work inner leg shaping (end of RS rows and beginning of WS rows) as follows: increase 1 stitch every 10th row once and every 4th row once, then when inner leg measures 2¹⁄₂"[6cm] from the beginning, ending with a RS row, shape crotch as follows:

NEXT ROW (WS) Bind off 3 stitches, purl to end.

Decrease 1 stitch at crotch edge on following 4th row 2 times and every 6th row once—38 (42, 46) stitches. Work even in stockinette stitch until piece measures 11¹⁄₂ (12, 12¹⁄₂)"[29 (30.5, 31.5)cm] from the beginning.

NEXT ROW (RS) Place marker at beginning and end of row and decrease 8 stitches evenly across. Place 30 (34, 38) stitches on holder.

Left Bottom Work as for the right bottom, reversing all shapings.

Back Waist Casing Place stitches from left back onto needle first and right back second, so inner leg seams meet—60 (68, 76) stitches.

Work 5 rows in stockinette stitch and leave stitches on needle. With 2nd pair of needles, pick up 60 (68, 76) stitches along marker row on inside back.

Work 5 rows in stockinette stitch.

NEXT ROW (RS) Place tip of right needle into the first stitch on both casing needles and knit both stitches at the same time. Slide off needle, continue to the end. Work even until the piece measures 13 (13¹⁄₂, 14)"[33 (34, 35.5)cm] from the top of the casing,

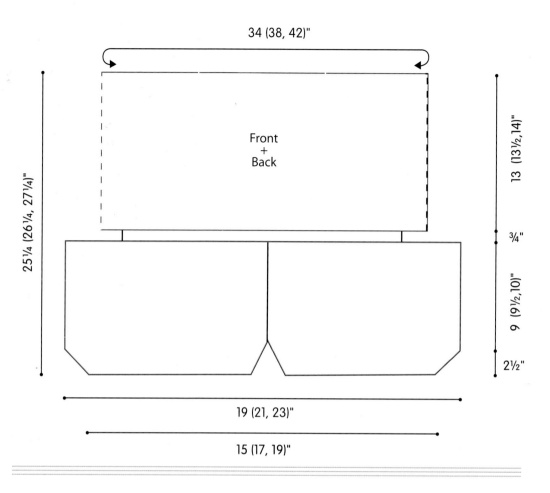

34 (38, 42)"

Front
+
Back

13 (13½, 14)"

¾"

25¼ (26¼, 27¼)"

9 (9½, 10)"

2½"

19 (21, 23)"

15 (17, 19)"

place marker at the beginning and end of the row. Place stitches on a holder.

FRONT

Bottom Right

SETUP ROW FOR COLORWORK Cast on 2 (6, 10) stitches in MC, 7 stitches in CC, 2 stitches in MC, 4 stitches in CC, 12 stitches in MC—27 (31, 35) stitches

In stockinette stitch, work side seam shaping (end of RS rows and beginning of WS rows) as follows: Increase 1 stitch on every row 2 times, every other row 4 (3, 2) times, every 4th row 1 time and every 6th row 0 (1, 2) time(s). At the same time, work inner leg shaping (beginning of RS rows and end of WS rows) as follows: Increase 1 stitch every 10th row once and every 4th row once, then when inner leg measures 2½"[6cm] from the beginning, ending with a WS row, shape crotch as follows:

NEXT ROW (RS) Bind off 3 stitches, knit to end.

Decrease 1 stitch at crotch edge on following 4th row 2 times and 6th row once—30 (34, 38) stitches.

Work even until the piece measures 10½ (11, 11½)"[26.5 (28, 29)cm] from the beginning. Place marker at the beginning and end of the row. Place stitches on a holder.

Left Bottom With MC, cast on 27 (31, 35) stitches. Work as for right bottom without intarsia stripes, reversing all shaping. Place marker at the beginning and end of the final row and place stitches on a holder.

Front Waist Casing Work as for the back waist casing, continue to work stripes up front. Inside casing is worked in MC—60 (68, 76) stitches.

TOP FRONT

NEXT ROW RS Increase 4 stitches evenly across the first 8 stitches of the row, work to the last 8 stitches of the row, increase 4 stitches evenly across the last 8 stitches—68 (76, 84) stitches. Work even until the piece measures 13 (13½, 14)"[33 (34, 35.5)cm] from the top of the casing, place marker at the beginning and end of the row. Place stitches on a holder. Place first 6 (10, 14) stitches onto stitch holder, work to the last 6 (10, 14) stitches, place these stitches onto a holder. Place 1 stitch onto holder at the beginning and end of every row 8 times. With circular needle, pick up all stitches for the back from the holder, and all stitches (including stitches from holders) across the front and work 5 rounds even. Bind off.

FINISHING

Do not block pieces. Sew the side seams. Sew each front and back inner leg seam. Sew the center seam from the front to the back using backstitch. Fold over top casing at markers and sew in place, leaving a 1"[2.5cm] opening for elastic. Insert a 29 (30, 31)"[73.5 (76, 78.5)cm] piece of elastic into bust casing. Overlap ends and stitch by machine or securely by hand with sewing needle and thread. Insert a 24 (25, 26)"[61 (63.5, 66)cm] piece of elastic into waist casing through one of the side seam openings. Overlap and sew the elastic ends. With yarn, vertical-weave casing opening over the secured elastic ends.

Trim With CC, cast on 6 stitches and work in stockinette stitch. Begin at back side seam, work until piece fits comfortably around the leg and up the side seam to waist. Fold trim in half and stitch RS in place first. Lap trim of front leg over starting point and stitch along side seam to waist. Lap trim to wrong side and stitch firmly in place.

CAP-SLEEVE MESH TANK

IT'S ALL ABOUT VINTAGE

Sizes
To fit S (M, L)

Finished Measurements
Bust to fit 34 (36, 38)"[86.5 (91.5, 96.5)cm]
Length 19¾ (21¼, 22¾)"[50 (54, 57.5)cm]

Materials
▤ 4 (5, 5) 1¾oz/50g 100yds/91m balls of Cascade Fixation (98.3% Cotton, 1.7% Elastic) in #4545 Melon

▤ One size G/6 [4mm] crochet hook

▤ Stitch markers

Gauge
6 loops x 16 rows = 4 x 4"[10 x 10cm] with size G/6 crochet hook in mesh pattern

This is a cute crochet-loop top that is worked in the round until you reach the armholes. You will work back and forth across the front, as well as the back of the tank, until you reach the neckline and shoulders. I recommend using stitch markers at the side seams to help distinguish them from the back. You can find these at any knitting store. If you don't have any, something as simple as a safety pin can make a good marker!

MESH CROCHET
ROUND 1 Chain 1, single crochet into 1st chain, *chain 6, skip 3 chain, single crochet into next chain, repeat from *, ending with skip last 3 chain, slip stitch in first single crochet.

ROUND 2 *Chain 6, single crochet in 4th chain (center of loop), repeat from * around.

Repeat round 2 for mesh pattern throughout.

BODY
Chain 168 (184, 200). Join in round by working slip stitch in first chain, taking care not to twist chain. Work 6 (10, 14) rounds in mesh crochet pattern—42 (46, 50) loops.

Place a marker at each end for sides—21 (23, 25) loops each for front and back. Carry markers up each round.

Decrease 1 loop at each marker (to decrease, skip 1 loop) on next round, and every 7th round 3 times more—34 (38, 42) loops. Work 14 rounds even.

Increase 1 loop (making 2 loops in 1 loop) at each marker on next round. Work 5 rounds even.

Repeat last 6 rounds once more—38 (42, 46) loops, 54 (58, 62) rounds have been worked.

Armhole Shaping Place a marker at each end for sides. There are 19 (21, 23) loops each for front and back. You will now be working back and forth in rows.

Top Back After marker, skip 1 loop (for armhole), work in pattern for 17 (19, 21) loops, skip 1 loop before marker (for armhole). Turn. Work 5 (7, 9) more rows even on back section only. Increase 1 loop at the beginning and end of every other row 3 times—23 (25, 27) loops. Work 4 rows even. Fasten off.

Left Front
NEXT ROW (RS) Begin with 19 (21, 23) loops

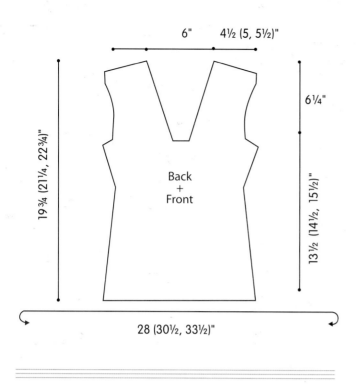

for front, skip first loop at armhole, work 8 (9, 10) loops across, ending at middle of center loop of neckline. Turn.

NEXT ROW Decrease 1 loop at neckline, work to end—7 (8, 9) loops. Increase 1 stitch at armhole by working a ½ loop (loop that will end in middle of loop below) in first loop at armhole and decrease 1 loop at neck to maintain 6½ (7½, 8½) loops for 10 (12, 14) more rows. Work 4 rows even. Without cutting the yarn, turn, chain 3. Connect the back to the front by working 1 single crochet into the back sleeve edge, *chain 3, work 1 single crochet in next loop of the front shoulder, chain 3, work 1 single crochet in the next loop for back, repeat from * for 6½ (7½, 8½) loops, leaving 9 loops for the back neck edge. Work the right side of the top front, reversing all shaping.

FINISHING

Work 2 rows around the armhole (skipping 2 loops underarm from front and back) as follows: *Chain 3, skip 3 stitches, double crochet, repeat from *, end chain 3. Work 1 row of single crochet around the neck edge, armholes, and bottom edge.

CUTE WITH A

BIKINI OR A SIMPLE TANK TOP UNDERNEATH.

RIBBON-YARN FLARED MINI

Sizes
To fit S (M, L, XL)

Finished Measurements
Low waist 32 (34, 36, 38)"[81 (86.5, 91.5, 96.5)cm]
Bottom edge 46 (48, 52, 56)"[117 (122, 132, 142)cm]

Materials
▨ 3 (4, 4, 5) 1¾oz/50g 81yds/74m balls of Cascade Yarns Egeo Ribbon (36% Polyester, 33% Nylon, 31% Cotton) in #509 Multicolor

▨ One Size H/8 [5mm] crochet hook

▨ One Size J/10 [6mm] crochet hook

▨ One 7"[18cm] invisible zipper

▨ Yarn needle

▨ Sewing thread

▨ Stitch markers

Gauge
15 single crochet x 16 rows = 4 x 4"[10 x 10cm] using J/10 hook

This simple low-rise skirt is a decorative blend of triple and single crochet rows. It has an "invisible" zipper sewn in at the side seam. If you need to shorten the zipper, create a bar tacking by stitching back and forth several times over the spot at which you'd like the zipper head to stop, and then just cut off the excess.

SKIRT
Beginning at waistband, with size H/8 hook, chain 121 (129, 143, 159). Work 1 single crochet in second chain from hook, and in each chain to end, chain 1, turn—120 (128, 142, 159) stitches. Work 8 rows even in single crochet. Change to size J/10 hook, chain 4. Turn.

Fold waistband in half, place marker at center.

NEXT (INCREASE) ROW Working in treble crochet, increase 20 (20, 21, 19) stitches evenly across (increase by working 2 treble crochet in 1 stitch)—140 (148, 163, 178) stitches.

NEXT ROW Increase 1 treble crochet (at the beginning and end of the row and once before and after the marker—4 stitches increased. Repeat the last row 3 times more.

Begin working treble crochet in the round, place marker at the second side opening and increase 1 stitch before and after each marker—4 stitches increased on next row. Repeat the last row 3 times more—172 (180, 195, 210) treble crochet. Work even in single crochet until skirt is the desired length. Fasten off.

FINISHING
Work 1 row of single crochet around the waistband and side opening. With sewing needle and thread, install the invisible zipper to the inside of the side opening, shortening the zipper, if necessary. (You can shorten the zipper by hand-stitching with needle and thread over the zipper teeth and cutting ½"[1.25cm] below the stitching.) Use small stitches to make sure the zipper is secure.

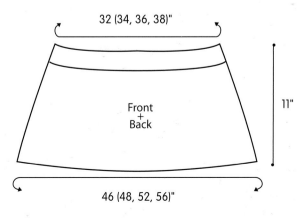

32 (34, 36, 38)"

Front + Back

11"

46 (48, 52, 56)"

DISCO TOP

Sizes
To fit XS (S, M, L)

Finished Measurements
Bust to fit 32 (34, 36, 38)"[81 (86.5, 91.5, 96.5)cm]
Length 14¼ (15¼, 16¼, 17¼)"[36 (38.5, 41, 43.5)cm]

Materials
▥ 1 (2, 2, 2) 40g 172m/187yd balls Diakeito Mim Diamist Lamenc (100% polyester) in #725 Multi (MC) and 1 ball in #727 (CC)

▥ One pair size 4 [3.5mm] needles

▥ One size B/1 [2.25mm] crochet hook

▥ Stitch holder

Gauge
21 stitches x 32 rows = 4 x 4"[10 x 10cm] on size 4 needles in stockinette stitch

Feel like dancing? You will when you wear this top. It has a decorative ladder stitch on the midriff and a columnar bra with top casings. The casings help create a double-tie effect for the halter. The top ties around the neck and at the back, but leaves most of the back bare.

LACE PATTERN
ROW 1 (RS) Knit 1,*(slip, slip, knit), yarn over twice, knit 2 together, knit 2, rep from *, end with knit 2 together, knit 1.

ROW 2 (WS) Purl 2, *purl 1, knit 1 into the yarn over, purl 4, repeat from *, end with purl 2.

Repeat rows 1 and 2 for lace pattern.

DOUBLE DECREASE (DBL) Slip 2 stitches knit-wise to right needle, knit 1, pass 2 slip stitches over.

FRONT
With MC, cast on 78 (90, 102, 114) stitches. Work lace pattern for 52 (56, 60, 64) rows.

NEXT (INCREASE) ROW (RS) Knit 1, *(slip, slip, knit), 3 yarn overs, knit 2 together, knit 2, repeat from *, end with knit 2 together, knit 1.

NEXT ROW (WS) Purl 2, *purl 1, knit 1, purl 1 into 3 yarn overs, purl 4, repeat from *, end with purl 2—91 (105, 119, 133) stitches. Work 4 rows in stockinette stitch.

UPPER BRA
Bind off 12 (15, 18, 21) stitches at the beginning of the next 2 rows—67 (75, 83, 91) stitches. Work 4 rows in stockinette stitch.

Left Cup
NEXT ROW (RS) Knit 33 (37, 41, 45) stitches, place remaining stitches on a holder.

NEXT ROW (WS) Purl 33 (37, 41, 45) stitches.

Work 4 (4, 2, 2) more rows in stockinette stitch on these 33 (37, 41, 45) stitches.

NEXT (DECREASE) ROW (RS) Knit 15 (17, 19, 21) stitches, place marker, DBL, knit 15 (17, 19, 21) stitches. Repeat DBL after marker every other row 0 (0, 0, 1) time, every 6th row 3 (1, 0, 0) time(s), every 4th row 0 (4, 6, 7) times—25 (25, 27, 27) stitches. Work bra section even until the piece measures 5 (5½, 6, 6½)"[12.5 (14, 15, 16.5)cm] from the armhole, place marker. Work 9 rows of stockinette stitch. Bind off.

Right Cup Place stitches from the holder onto the left needle.

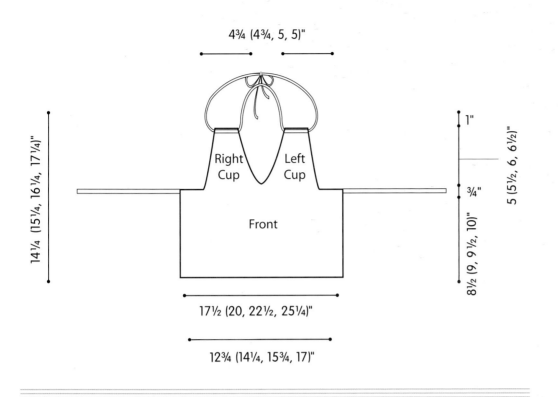

4¾ (4¾, 5, 5)"

14¼ (15¼, 16¼, 17¼)"

Right Cup

Left Cup

Front

1"

¾"

5 (5½, 6, 6½)"

8½ (9, 9½, 10)"

17½ (20, 22½, 25¼)"

12¾ (14¼, 15¾, 17)"

NEXT ROW (RS) Bind off the center stitch. Work as for the first bra section on remaining 33 (37, 41, 45) stitches. Bind off.

FINISHING
With CC and crochet hook, begin at top left neckline: Chain 1, 3 single crochet, double crochet around inner neckline, end with 3 single crochet. Begin at top right cup, 3 single crochet, double crochet to bottom, work lace pattern (instructions follow) across the bottom, work double crochet up the left side, end with 3 single crochet.

LACE PATTERN
ROW 1 Double crochet across the row—3 double crochet for every stockinette stitch section, 2 double crochet for every double yarn over.

ROW 2 *Double crochet, chain 1, skip 1 double crochet from previous row, repeat from *, end with double crochet.

ROW 3 (Picot Edge) *Single crochet, chain 3, single crochet into double crochet, chain 2, repeat from *, end with single crochet. Fasten off.

Fold over top edge of bra casing and sew to WS along marked row.

Neckline Strap
ROW 1 With CC, chain 6, double crochet in 4th chain from hook, double crochet in each of last 2 chain, turn.

ROW 2 Chain 3, double crochet in each double crochet, turn.

Repeat row 2 until strap measures 60"[152cm]. Fasten off. Work second strap same as the first. Thread straps through casings.

Side Strap
ROW 1 With CC, chain 7, double crochet in 4th chain from hook, double crochet in each of last 3 chains, turn.

ROW 2 Chain 3, double crochet in each double crochet, turn.

Repeat row 2 until strap measures 19"[48cm]. Fasten off. Attach to side edge. Work second strap same as the first.

V-NECK SWEATER DRESS

Sizes
To fit XS (S, M, L)

Finished Measurements
Bust 33 (35, 37, 39)"[84 (89, 94, 99)cm]
Bottom Width (widest part) 38 (40, 42, 44)"[96.5 (101.5, 106.5, 111.5)cm]
Upper arm 14 (14½, 15, 16)"[35.5 (37, 38, 40.5)cm]

Materials
▦ 5 (5, 6, 6) 1.4 oz/40g 126yds/115m balls each of Diakeito Silklame (58% wool, 40% silk, 2% polyester) in #903 Lilac (A), #904 Mauve (B), #902 Vanilla (C)

▦ One pair each sizes 4 [3.5mm] and 5 [3.75mm] needles

▦ One crochet hook size D/4 [3.25m]

▦ Stitch markers

Gauge
22 stitches x 32 rows = 4 x 4"[10 x 10 cm] on size 5 needles in stockinette stitch

This knit, striped dress is fun to wear and simple to knit. It has cute flared sleeves and a deep sexy V-neck front and back. If you want to lengthen this minidress so that it falls below your knees, decrease every 25th row (instead of every 20th row). Don't forget to stock up on extra yarn in case you decide to go longer.

BACK
With smaller needles and A, cast on 104 (110, 116, 122) stitches. Work in knit 1, purl 1 rib for 4 rows. Change to larger needles, work in stockinette stitch and stripe pattern as follows: 14 rows A, 14 rows B and 14 rows C; repeat the color pattern throughout. Decrease 1 stitch at the beginning and end of every 20th row 5 times and then every 18th row twice—90 (96, 102, 108) stitches. Work even until the back measures 26 (26½, 27, 27½)"[66 (67.5, 68.5, 70)cm], ending with a WS row.

Armhole Shaping
Bind off 5 (5, 6, 7) stitches at the beginning of the next 2 rows—80 (86, 90, 94) stitches.

NEXT ROW (RS) Knit 2, (slip, slip, knit), work to the last 4 stitches, knit 2 together, knit 2. Repeat decrease row every other row 5 times more. At the same time, when piece measures 27 (27¼, 27¾, 28¼)"[68.5 (69, 70.5, 71.5)cm] from the beginning, ending with a WS row, begin neck shaping.

Neck Shaping Knit to 6 center stitches, knit 2 together, place marker, knit 4, place marker, (slip, slip, knit), knit to end.

NEXT ROW Purl.

NEXT ROW (RS) Knit to first marker, knit 2 together, pass marker, knit 2, join another ball of yarn, knit 2, pass marker, (slip, slip, knit), knit to end. Working both sides at the same time, continue to decrease 1 stitch before first marker and 1 stitch after second marker every RS row until you have 10 stitches remaining each side. When length measures 33 (33¾, 34½, 35¼)"[84 (85.5, 87.5, 89.5)cm] from beginning, bind off.

FRONT
Work as for the back until the piece measures 24¾ (25¼, 25¾, 26¼)"[63 (64, 65.5,

66.5)cm] from the beginning. Work the neckline shaping until you have 10 stitches remaining at each shoulder. Work even until the piece measures the same as for the back, bind off.

SLEEVES

With smaller needles and A, cast on 66 (68, 70, 72) stitches. Work 4 rows of knit 1, purl 1 rib. With larger needles and in stockinette stitch, continue in stripe pattern as for back. Decrease 1 stitch at the beginning and end of every 4th row 9 times—48 (50, 52, 54) stitches. Work even until the piece measures 6"[15cm] from the beginning. Increase 1 stitch at the beginning and end of every 6th row 2 (1, 1, 1) times and every 4th row 12

(13, 14, 15) times—76 (78, 82, 86) stitches. Work even until the piece measures 14½ (14¾, 15, 15¼)"[37 (37.5, 38, 38.5)cm] from the beginning, ending with a WS row.

Cap Shaping Bind off 5 (5, 6, 7) stitches at the beginning of the next 2 rows. Decrease 1 stitch at the beginning and end of every other row 6 times. Decrease 1 stitch at the beginning and end of every row 19 (20, 21, 22) times. Bind off remaining 16 stitches.

FINISHING

Block pieces. Sew the shoulder seams. Single crochet around the neck edge if desired for smooth neckline. Sew the sleeves to armholes. Sew the side and sleeve seams.

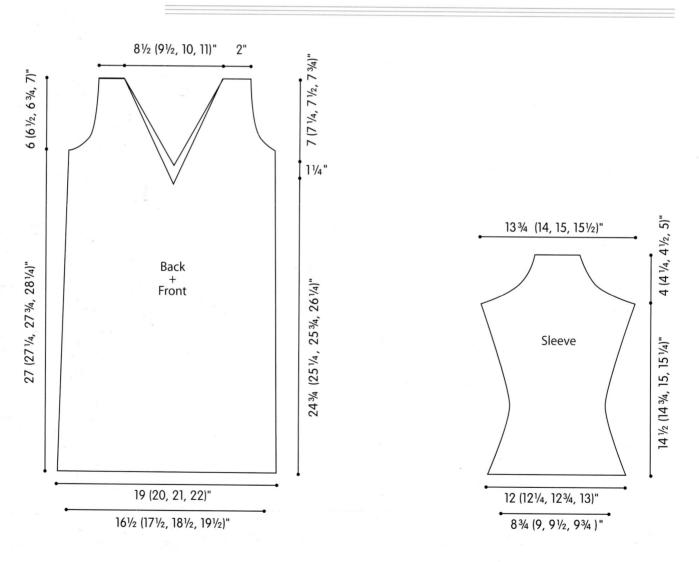

HEART BABYDOLL HALTER DRESS

Sizes
To fit S (M, L)

Finished Measurements
Bust cup width 9 (10¼, 11)"[23 (26, 28)cm]
Waist 26 (28, 30)"[66 (71, 76)cm]
Length of skirt 18¾ (19¾, 20¾)"[47.5 (50, 53)cm]
Total Length 28 (30, 32)"[71 (76, 81)cm]

Materials
▤ 8 (9, 10) 1.4oz/40g 140 yds/128m balls of Diakeito Diasantafe (50% Viscose, 34% Ramide, 16% Nylon) #519 Aqua Multi

▤ One pair size 4 [3.5mm] knitting needles

▤ One size C/2 [2.75mm] crochet hook

▤ ⅝yd[0.5m] of ¼"[6mm] nylon swimwear elastic

▤ Stitch markers

Gauge
27 stitches x 32 rows = 4 x 4"[10 x 10cm] on size 4 needles in stockinette stitch

This little number is a more intricately knit dress, with lace hearts on the front and back of the skirt. I recommend using lots of stitch markers to help you keep your place while you're knitting the hearts. This dress finishes easily in flat stockinette drawstrings with edges that curl and don't need to be sewn.

SKIRT

Back Cast on 186 (199, 216) stitches. Working in stockinette stitch, decrease 1 stitch at the beginning and end of every 4th row 38 (38, 40) times, then every 6th row 1 time—108 (121, 134) stitches.

Setup Row for Motifs
After working 10 (10, 14) rows from the beginning, and there are 182 (195, 210) stitches on the needle, begin working motifs as follows:

NEXT ROW (RS) Knit 4 (7, 11) stitches, place marker (pm), *work row 1 of motif A, pm, knit 10 (11, 12) stitches, repeat from * 7 times more, end with knit 4 (7, 11) stitches rather than knit 10 (11, 12). When all rows of motif A are complete, work 8 (10, 10) rows while maintaining decreases and keeping markers

in place. Begin working row 1 of motif B on all stitches between markers. Work 8 (10, 10) rows when motif B is complete.

Continue working 8 (10, 10) rows between completed motifs, but alternating motif A with B up entire length of skirt. *Only work half or full motifs while decreasing for skirt. If there are not enough stitches to work a full or half motif, work in stockinette stitch. When back skirt measures 18¾ (19¾, 20¾)"[47.5 (50, 52.5)cm] from the beginning, bind off loosely.

Front Work as for the back.

BODICE
Lightly block the skirt pieces. Sew the side seams. Begin 1"[2.5cm] behind back skirt side seam and ending 1"[2.5cm] behind the second skirt side seam, pick up and knit 109 (121, 133) stitches. Work 10 rows even. Begin decreasing 2 stitches at the beginning and end of every row 3 (6, 9) times. Decrease 3 stitches at the beginning and end of every row 10 times. Finish by decreasing 2 stitches at the beginning and end of every row 9 times until one stitch remains. Bind off.

Left Bust Cup Begin at top corner of bodice in back, pick up and knit 61 (69, 77) stitches to center.

WHAT A SWEET SUNDRESS WITH

PEEK-A-BOO HEARTS!

MOTIF A

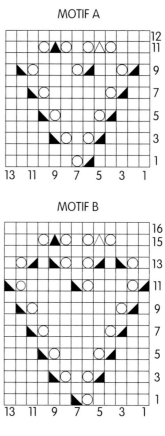

MOTIF B

STITCH KEY

☐ Knit on RS rows, purl on WS rows

◖ Yarn over

◣ Knit 2 together

◣ Slip 1 (knitwise), knit 1, pass slip stitch over

△ Skip 1, knit 2 together, pass slip stitch over

◣ Knit 2 together, return stitch to left needle, pass next stitch over it, slip stitch back to right needle

We had to throw in a cute A-line halter dress. This "Heart Babydoll Halter Dress" has the perfect amount of peek-a-boo detail in the heart-shaped stitch and good support on the top. The Diakeito space-dyed yarn is soft and has the perfect drape for this dress. If you prefer, make it super short and wear it as a top over jeans.

Purl.

Decrease 1 stitch at the beginning and end of the next row and every other row until 5 stitches remain. Work even in stockinette stitch for 13 (14, 15)"[33 (35.5, 38)cm] to make curling strap. Bind off. Repeat for right bust cup.

Bodice Side Straps Pick up and knit 8 stitches along side edge of bodice and work in stockinette stitch for 17 (18, 19)"[43 (46, 48)cm]. Bind off.

FINISHING

Lightly block the bodice and cups. With the crochet hook, work 1 row of single crochet around all edges of the bodice strap and the bottom edge of the skirt. Work a second row around the bottom edge of the skirt as follows: *1 single crochet, chain 4, skip 3 stitches, repeat from * to end. Fasten off. Work 1 row of single crochet around the top of the back skirt, carry a piece of elastic as a running thread to hide between stitches. Try it on for the best fit. Secure the ends of the elastic. Work 1 row of scallop crochet around the top edge of the back skirt as follows: *1 single crochet, chain 2, skip 1 stitch, repeat from * to end. Fasten off. Begin above the side strap, work 1 row of filet crochet around all bust cup edges as follows: chain 4, skip 1,*1 double crochet, chain 1, skip 1, repeat from * to end. Work a second row of small scallop stitch as for the back along the filet crochet edges.

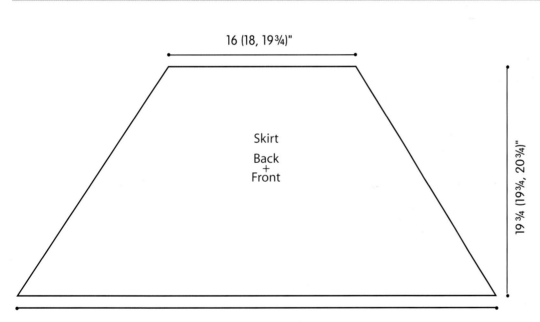

16 (18, 19¾)"

Skirt

Back
+
Front

19¾ (19¾, 20¾)"

27½ (29½, 32)"

CHAPTER 3

COZY HOMEBODIES

The art of knitting is sometimes accused of being old-fashioned and grannyish. But guess what? Those days are over. As I am sure you've noticed, some of the most fashionable, sexy women in the world have picked up knitting needles and have begun creating their own designs. Isn't it an obvious next step for us all to start knitting sexier things? For instance, doesn't a soft, fluffy camisole-and-panty set sound ten times more intriguing to knit than a winter sweater? How about trying your needles on a lace-stitch nightgown instead of a matching beanie and scarf? (I think you know which would be more fun.)

Knitting is a personal pursuit that's dear to our hearts, but it's quite sensual, too. Your fingers are in constant touch with the yarn and the needles, and each stitch takes TLC and attention. And there's nothing more personal and sensual than knitting your own nightie. Wear the lingerie-inspired designs in this chapter around the house when you want to feel especially sexy and pampered. (Or when you want to tease your honey a bit.)

In case you haven't picked up on it yet, this book is about sexy knits, not granny knits, so go for it, girlfriend!

COZY SLEEPER

Sizes
To fit XS (S, M, L)

Finished Measurements
Bust at underarm, buttoned 32 (35, 37, 39)"[81 (89, 94, 99)cm]
Length 23 (23$\frac{1}{2}$, 24$\frac{1}{4}$, 24$\frac{3}{4}$)"[58.5 (59.5, 61.5, 63)cm]
Hip 33 (36, 38, 40)"[84 (91.5, 96.5, 101.5)cm]

Materials
▧ 6 (7, 7, 8)$\frac{7}{8}$oz/25g balls (each approximately 116yds/106m) of Anny Blatt Angora Super (70% Angora, 30% Wool) in #164 Dragee.

▧ One pair each of needles in sizes 3 [3.25mm] and 5 [3.75mm]

▧ Eight $\frac{3}{8}$"[10mm] buttons

▧ Rainbow elastic

Gauge
22 stitches and 33 rows = 4 x 4"[10 x 10cm] with size 5 needles over stockinette stitch

This all-over, easy-to-knit stockinette sleeper has a full fashion decrease at the side seams, and it's super soft. It has simple eyelet buttonholes; have fun picking small vintage buttons that you love. The leg openings feature knit-in rainbow elastic.

BACK
With larger needles cast on 10 stitches. Work 10 rows in stockinette stitch.

Increase 1 stitch at the beginning and end of the next row and every other row once more—14 stitches. Purl next row.

Loosely cast on at the end of the next row and at the end of every following row 7 (11, 15, 21) stitches twice, 12 (16, 20, 20) stitches twice, 14 (8, 6, 6) stitches twice, and 6 (8, 6, 6) stitches twice—92 (100, 108, 120) stitches. Work even for 18 (20, 22, 24) rows.

DECREASE ROW (RS) Knit 4, [slip, slip, knit], knit to last 6 stitches, knit 2 together, knit 4. Repeat decrease row every 6th row 4 times, every 4th row 2 (2, 2, 1) times, every other row 3 (3, 3, 6) times—72 (80, 88, 96) stitches. Work even over next 22 rows.

INCREASE ROW (RS) Knit 4, M1 (make 1) by placing yarn running in front of the next stitch onto left needle and knit into the back of it, knit to last 4 stitches, M1, knit 4. Work increase row every 4th row 3 (3, 3, 2) times more. Work increase row every other row 5 (5, 4, 4) times—90 (98, 104, 110) stitches.

Armhole Shaping When piece measures 16$\frac{3}{4}$ (17, 17$\frac{1}{4}$, 17$\frac{1}{2}$)"[42.5 (43, 43.5, 44.5)cm] from beginning, ending with a WS row, bind off 8 (9, 9, 10) stitches at the beginning of the next 2 rows. Decrease 1 stitch at the beginning and end of the next row, every other row 7 times, and then every 4th row 3 times. At the same time and when piece measures 18$\frac{3}{4}$ (19, 19$\frac{1}{4}$, 19$\frac{1}{2}$)"[47.5 (48, 49, 49.5)cm] from beginning, work neckline as follows:

Neckline Bind off center 28 (34, 40, 44) stitches. Join 2nd ball of yarn. Decrease 1 stitch on right and left side of each neck edge every row 4 times, and then every other row 5 times. When piece measures 20$\frac{1}{2}$ (20$\frac{3}{4}$, 21, 21$\frac{1}{4}$)"[52 (52.5, 53.5, 54)cm] from beginning, bind off remaining 3 stitches each side for tabs.

FRONT
Work as for the back until the piece measures 7$\frac{1}{2}$"[19cm] from the beginning.

NEXT ROW (RS) Place the center 4 stitches on a holder. Join a 2nd ball of yarn and continue to work shapings as for the back, beginning armhole shaping as for the back. At the same time, begin neck shaping as follows: Bind off 6 (9, 12, 14) stitches on both sides of center neck edge, decrease 1 stitch every row 7 times, every other row 7 times, and every 4th row 1 time. Bind off when the front is the same length as the back.

Left Button Band Cast on 5 stitches and work in knit 1, purl 1 rib, until the piece measures the same length as the front opening. Bind off in rib.

Right Buttonhole Band With smaller needles, place 4 stitches from the holder to the left-hand needle.

Work in knit 1, purl 1 rib over the 4 stitches beginning with a knit. Increase 1 stitch in stockinette stitch—5 stitches. Work in rib for 6 rows.

BUTTONHOLE ROW Knit 1, yarn over, knit 2 together, knit 1. Work piece until it is the same length as the front opening. At the same time, work remaining buttonholes as follows: Work top buttonhole ¼"[6mm] from top of neckline, and remaining 6 buttonholes evenly spaced. Bind off in rib.

FINISHING

Block the pieces according to label recommendations. Sew the side seams. With smaller needles, pick up and knit 126 (134, 142, 154) across the leg opening. Work in knit 1, purl 1 rib, carrying elastic along purl stitches, for 4 rows. Bind off loosely in rib. Repeat for the other leg opening. Sew the front and back together at the crotch. Sew the bands to the front opening edges. Slip stitch the bottom edges of both bands together on WS. Sew on buttons.

Straps Cast on 5 stitches and work in knit 1, purl 1 rib, until the piece fits from the side seam to the center top of back tab, place the stitches onto a holder. Repeat the process for remaining armholes of front and back. Cast on 5 stitches and repeat for the front bands from the center front to the top of the tab and from tab to tab across the center back. Sew all the bands in place, adjust length of bands, if necessary, for best fit. For each front strap, place all 10 stitches from holders onto needles. Decrease center knit stitches to create 1 center knit stitch: 1 (slip, slip, knit) for right side strap, and knit 2 together for left strap. Work knit 1, purl 1 rib on remaining stitches until piece measures 23 (23½, 24¼, 24¾)"[58.5 (59.5, 61.5, 63)cm]. Bind off in rib. Repeat process for back straps until they are the same length as the front. Sew the straps together at the shoulders.

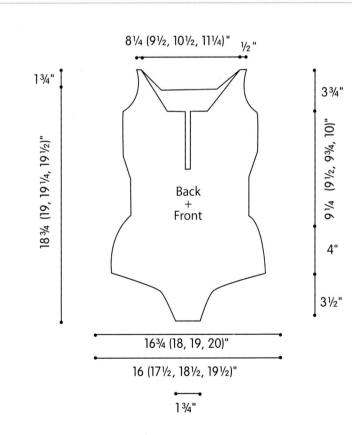

8¼ (9½, 10½, 11¼) " ½ "

1¾ "

18¾ (19, 19¼, 19½)"

3¾ "

9¼ (9½, 9¾, 10)"

4"

Back + Front

3½ "

16¾ (18, 19, 20)"

16 (17½, 18½, 19½)"

1¾ "

WINTER TANK

Sizes
To fit S (M, L, XL)

Finished Measurements
(Very close fitting)
Bust stretches to fit 34
(36, 38, 40)"[86.5 (91.5,
96.5, 101.5)cm]
Bottom width 16 (17, 19½,
22)"[40.5 (43, 49.5,
56)cm]
Length 21¼ (22½, 23¼,
24)"[54 (57, 59, 61)cm]

Materials
▤ 5 (5, 6, 6) 1¾oz/50g
165yds/150m balls each
Lana Grossa Estivo (60%
Baumuolle Cotton, 40%
Microfiber Polymide) in
#014 Pink (MC), and 1 ball
of #018, Aqua (CC)

▤ One pair size 5
[3.75mm] needles

▤ One size 3 [3.25mm]
circular needle, 24"[61cm]

▤ One size F/5 [3.75mm]
crochet hook

▤ Stitch markers

Gauge
24 stitches x 36 rows = 4
x 4"[10 x 10cm] with size 5
needles over stockinette
stitch

This pink fluffy winter tank has an ultra-low V-neck front and back that are knit in contrasting colors of yarn. There are decreases at the center of the V-neck to create a neat edge, and the bottom edge has lovely picot trim.

BACK
With larger needles and MC, cast on 97 (103, 117, 133) stitches. Work in stockinette stitch for 3 (3½, 4, 4)"[7.5 (9, 10, 10)cm]. Decrease 1 stitch at the beginning and end of every other row 0 (0, 0, 3) times, every 4th row 6 (6, 6, 6) times—85 (91, 105, 115) stitches. Work even until the piece measures 12 (12½, 12¾, 13¼)"[30.5 (31.5, 32.5, 33.5)cm] from the beginning.

Neckline
NEXT ROW (RS) Knit 42 (45, 52, 57) stitches, join a 2nd ball of yarn and bind off center stitch, knit 42 (45, 52, 57) stitches. Working both sides of neck at the same time, purl 1 row.

NEXT ROW (RS) Decrease 1 stitch at each neck edge every other row 23 (24, 27, 29) times. At the same time, when the piece measures 14¾ (15½, 15¾, 16¼)"[37.5 (39.5, 40, 41)cm] from the beginning, decrease for armhole as follows:

Armhole Shaping
Bind off 5 (6, 6, 8) stitches at the beginning of the next 2 rows. Decrease 1 stitch every other row at armhole 8 (9, 13, 14) times. Continue to decrease at neck and armhole edges until 6 stitches remain. Work even until the piece measures 21¼ (22½, 23¼, 24)"[54 (57, 59, 61)cm] from the beginning. Bind off.

FRONT
Work same as for the back.

FINISHING
Back V-Neck With circular needle and CC (carry elastic along purl stitches, if desired), begin at shoulder and pick up and knit 84 (90, 94, 98) stitches to center, place marker, pick up 1 stitch at center, place marker, pick up 84 (90, 94, 98) stitches to opposite shoulder. Work 3 rows of knit 1, purl 1 rib, decreasing 1 stitch before first marker and 1 stitch after second marker every row. Bind off in pattern. Work front V-neck same as the back. Sew the shoulder seams.

Armholes With circular needle and CC, pick up 126 (136, 148, 160) stitches along armhole edge. Do not join.

Work 3 rows of knit 1, purl 1 rib while

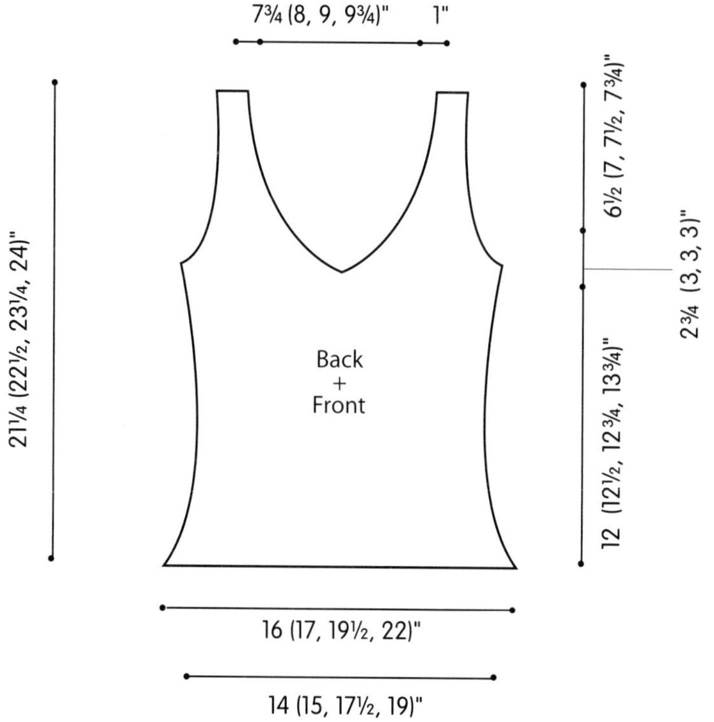
7¾ (8, 9, 9¾)"
1"
21¼ (22½, 23¼, 24)"
6½ (7, 7½, 7¾)"
2¾ (3, 3, 3)"
12 (12½, 12¾, 13¾)"
Back + Front
16 (17, 19½, 22)"
14 (15, 17½, 19)"

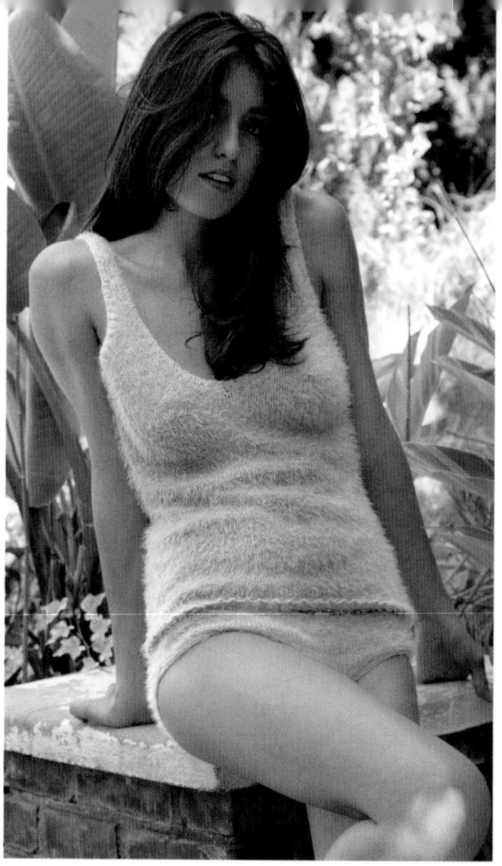

Knit this matching "Winter Tank & Hipster Set" in any color or striped variation in Lana Grossa super-soft yarn. The fabric is cuddly, sweet, and ultra flirtatious. The low-rider bottoms and deep V-neck tank will warm up even the chilliest winter night.

carrying rainbow elastic across purl stitches. Bind off in pattern. Sew side seams.

Picot Edging With crochet hook, work 1 row of single crochet around bottom edge, chain 1, turn.

NEXT ROUND Work 1 single crochet in first single crochet, *chain 3, work 1 single crochet in first chain stitch from hook, work single crochet in next 2 single crochet, repeat from *, end with 1 single crochet. Fasten off.

HIPSTERS

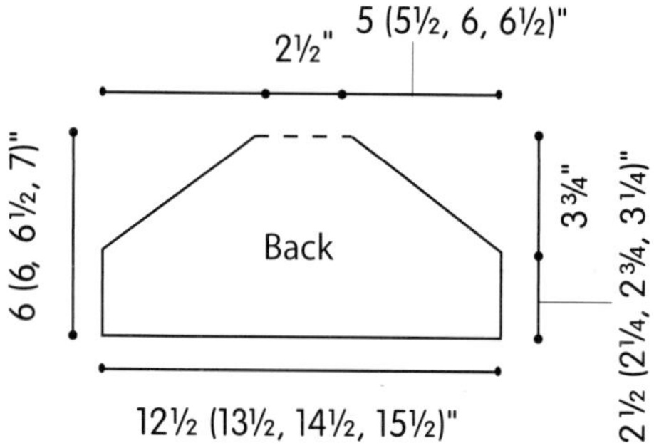
2½"
5 (5½, 6, 6½)"
6 (6, 6½, 7)"
Back
3¾"
2½ (2¼, 2¾, 3¼)"
12½ (13½, 14½, 15½)"

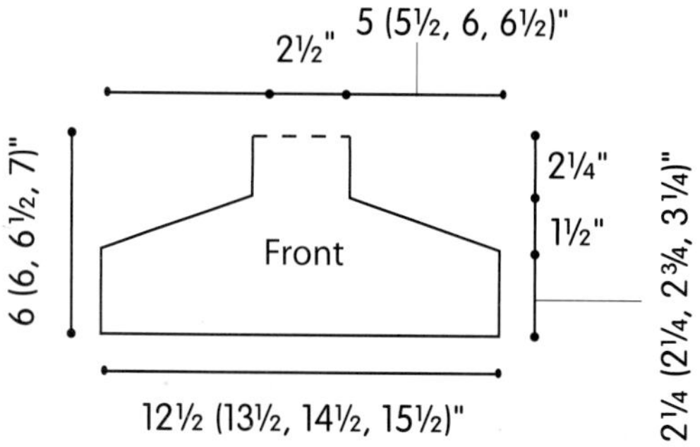
2½"
5 (5½, 6, 6½)"
6 (6, 6½, 7)"
Front
2¼"
1½"
2¼ (2¼, 2¾, 3¼)"
12½ (13½, 14½, 15½)"

Sizes

To fit S (M, L, XL)

Finished Measurements

Hip to fit 34 (36, 38, 40)"[86 (91.5, 96.5, 101.5)cm]

Materials

▨ 1 (1, 2, 2) 1¾oz/50g 164yds/150m balls Lana Grossa Estivo (60% Bumuolle Cotton, 40% Microfiber Polymide) in #018 Aqua (MC), and 1 ball of #014, Pink (CC)

▨ One pair size 4 [3.25mm] needles

▨ Rainbow elastic

▨ Stitch markers

▨ Stitch holders

Gauge

26 stitches x 40 rows = 4 x 4"[10 x 10cm] with size 4 needles over stockinette stitch

---

These panties offer versatile comfort and basic shaping, with rows of multiple-contrast stripes. Knit clear elastic in the leg openings to allow for some give.

OPTIONAL STRIPE PATTERN

Work stripes of color at the same time as any increases or decreases: After cast-on, work 6 rows of MC, 4 rows of CC, 4 rows of MC, 4 rows CC, 4 rows of MC, 6 rows of CC, work in MC to end.

NOTE Casting on with a needle 1 to 2 sizes larger than needle used to obtain gauge is recommended. Change to needle used to obtain gauge to work pattern throughout. Using a larger needle will eliminate the need for a loose cast-on.

FRONT

Loosely cast on 82 (88, 94, 100) stitches.

NEXT ROW (WS) Purl 1 row. Work in stockinette stitch until the piece measures 2¼ (2¼, 2¾, 3¼)"[5.5 (5.5, 7, 8.5)cm] from beginning, ending with a WS row. Bind off 22 (25, 28, 31) stitches at the beginning of the next 2 rows—38 stitches.

NEXT (DECREASE) ROW (RS) Knit 1, knit 2 together, work to last 3 stitches, (slip, slip, knit), knit 1.

NEXT ROW (WS) Purl. Repeat last 2 rows twice—32 stitches. Work decrease row every row 8 times (to work decrease on WS: purl 1, purl 2 together, work to last 3 stitches, purl 2 together through back loop, purl 1)—16 stitches. Place marker. Work even in stockinette stitch until the piece

measures 2¼"[5.5cm] from the marker, place stitches on a holder.

BACK

Work as for the front until the piece measures 2¼ (2¼, 2¾, 3¼)"[5.5 (5.5, 7, 8.5)cm] from the beginning.

NEXT (DECREASE) ROW (RS) Knit 1, knit 2 together, work to last 3 stitches, (slip, slip, knit), knit 1.

NEXT ROW (WS) Purl. Repeat the last 2 rows 13 (12, 8, 8) times more—54 (62, 76, 82) stitches.

NEXT ROW (RS) Knit 1, knit 2 together, knit 1, knit 2 together, work to last 6 stitches, (slip, slip, knit), knit 1, (slip, slip, knit), knit 1—50 (58, 72, 78) stitches.

NEXT ROW Purl. Repeat the last 2 rows 1 (1, 3, 1) time(s).

NEXT ROW Knit 1, knit 2 together, knit 1, knit 2 together, knit 1, knit 2 together, work to last 9 stitches, (slip, slip, knit), knit 1, (slip, slip, knit), knit 1, (slip, slip, knit), knit 1—40 (48, 54, 68) stitches.

NEXT ROW Purl. Repeat the last 2 rows 2 (3, 4, 6) times. Bind off 6 (7, 7, 8) stitches at the beginning of the next 2 rows—16 stitches. Place stitches on a holder.

FINISHING

Sew the side seams. Use three-needle bind-off to connect front and back stitches from the holders. In CC, work 1 row of single crochet, carrying elastic for extra stability around waist and leg openings.

BATHING BEAUTY ROBE

Sizes
To fit S (M, L, XL)

Finished Measurements
Bust and Hip 40 (43, 46, 50)"[101.5 (109, 117, 127)cm]
Length 28 (29½, 30½, 32)"[71 (75, 77.5, 81)cm]
Upper arm 16 (17, 18, 19)"[40.5 (43, 45.5, 48.5)cm]

Materials
▥ 15 (17, 18, 19) 1¾oz/50g 115yds/105m balls Wendy Velvet Touch (100% Nylon Polymide) in #1206 Yellow

▥ One pair each of sizes 6 [4mm] and 7 [4.5mm] needles

▥ One size F/5 [3.75mm] crochet hook

▥ Stitch markers

Gauge
19 stitches x 24 rows = 4 x 4"[10 x 10cm] with size 7 needles over stockinette stitch

Basic and fast, this must-have robe is knitted with a shawl collar and detached belt. If you want to give it an extra touch, add belt loops with single crochet chains, using contrasting yarn. The style is fuller in the back than in the front for superb, slouchy-yet-feminine Sunday morning lounging.

BACK

With larger needles, loosely cast on 95 (103, 109, 119) stitches. Work in stockinette stitch until the piece measures 20 (21, 21½, 22½)"[51 (53.5, 54.5, 57)cm] from the beginning, place marker at the beginning and end of the row. Work even until piece measures 28 (29½, 30½, 32)"[71 (75, 77.5, 81)]cm from the beginning. Bind off.

LEFT FRONT

With larger needles, loosely cast on 47 (51, 54, 59) stitches. Work in stockinette stitch until the piece measures 14 (15⅝, 16⅝, 18)"[35.5 (39.5, 42, 46)]cm from the beginning, begin neckline shaping.

Neckline Shaping

NEXT ROW (RS) Decrease row. Work to last 2 stitches, decrease 1. Repeat decrease row at front neckline edge (end of row RS) every

4th row 9 (9, 19, 19) times more, and then every 6th row 7 (7, 0, 0) times. Work as for the back, placing marker at armhole. Work even until the piece is the same length as the back. Bind off.

RIGHT FRONT

Work same as for the Left Front, reversing shaping.

SLEEVES

With larger needles, cast on 76 (80, 86, 90) stitches. Work in stockinette stitch until the piece measures 19 (19½, 20, 20)"[48 (49.5, 51, 51)cm] from the beginning. Bind off.

BELT

With smaller needles, cast on 12 stitches. Work in stockinette stitch until the piece measures 68 (68, 72, 72)"[172.5 (172.5, 183, 183)cm], bind off. With RS facing, work 1 row of single crochet around belt edge.

FINISHING

Block pieces. Sew the front to the back at the shoulders. Sew the sleeves to the armholes. Sew side and sleeve seams.

Garter Stitch Collar With RS facing and smaller needles, pick up 2 stitches at beginning of right front neck edge.

YOU'LL LIVE IN THIS LUSH ROBE AT HOME.

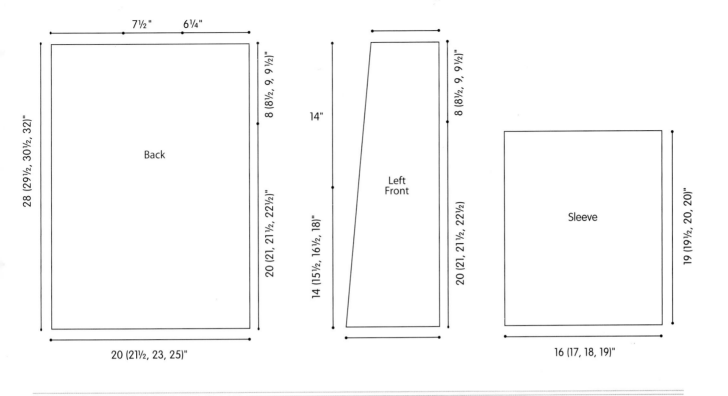

INCREASE ROW 1 (RS) Knit stitches on needle to end, pick up stitch from neck edge.

ROW 2 Knit all stitches on needle to end. Repeat rows 1 and 2 until you have 26 stitches.

NEXT ROW (RS) Knit to end, pick up 1 stitch from neck edge—27 stitches.

NEXT ROW (WS) Slip 1 (picked-up stitch), knit 1, pass slipped stitch over, knit to end—26 stitches. Continue working last two rows until there is 5¼"[13.5cm] remaining

to beginning of front neck edge. Work decrease rows as follows:

DECREASE ROW 1 (RS) Knit stitches on needle to end, pick up stitch from neck edge.

ROW 2 (WS) Slip 1, knit 2 together, pass slipped stitch over, knit to end. Continue until 2 stitches remain. Bind off. Sew the remaining stitches neatly to neck edge.

Work 1 row of single crochet around edge of collar.

We all need a cozy bathrobe for lazy days, when all we need to do is catch up on our entertainment news. This "Bathing Beauty" robe, knit in Wendy's Peter Pan Velvet Touch, is luxurious enough for royalty. Treat yourself right!

BRING ON THE TLC AND BE QUEEN

FOR A DAY—YOU DESERVE IT.

MESH LONG NIGHTGOWN

Sizes
To fit S (M, L, XL)

Measurements
Bust/Hip 34 (36, 38, 40)"[86.5 (91.5, 96.5, 101.5)cm]
Length 61 (61, 61½, 61½)"[155 (155, 156, 156)cm]

Materials
▥ 14 (16, 18, 20) 1¾oz/50g, 114yds/105m balls GGH Scarlett (100% Cotton) in color #006 Chocolate

▥ Two pairs size 4 [3.5mm] needles

▥ One size E/4 [3.5mm] crochet hook

▥ Stitch markers

Gauge
22 stitches x 30 rows = 4 x 4"[10 x 10cm] with size 4 needles over stockinette stitch

This dramatic, femme-fatale nightie is knit in stockinette stitch at the top of the front and back, then it features mesh open stitch from the bottom of the bustline all the way down to the hem. It has a long keyhole center-front with a drawstring that laces through the center mesh.

SIMPLE MESH
ROW 1 Knit 1, *knit 2 together, yarn over, repeat from *, end knit 1.

ROWS 2 AND 4 Purl.

ROW 3 *Knit 2 together, yarn over, repeat from *, end knit 2.

BACK
Cast on 110 (114, 120, 124) stitches. Work in simple mesh for 5"[12.5cm]. Keeping in pattern, decrease 1 stitch at the beginning and end of every 16th row 13 (13, 6, 6) times, and every 14th row 0 (0, 8, 8) times—84 (88, 92, 96) stitches. Work even until the piece measures 47"[119.5cm] from the beginning.

NEXT ROW (RS) (Place a marker at the beginning and end of row.) In stockinette stitch, increase 10 (10, 12, 14) stitches evenly across row—94 (98, 104, 110) stitches.

Casing Work 5 rows even. With a third needle, pick up and knit 94 (98, 104, 110) stitches on WS along marked row, work 5 rows in stockinette stitch even until casing row is even with back.

NEXT ROW (RS) Insert right-hand needle into first stitch of each of 2 left-hand needles as if to knit, knit both stitches at the same time. Continue across row to end to form casing—94 (98, 104, 110) stitches. Purl 1 row.

Neckline Shaping
NEXT ROW (RS) Knit 46 (48, 51, 54) stitches, bind off center 2 stitches, join a 2nd ball of yarn, knit 46 (48, 51, 54) stitches. Working both sides at the same time, work 5 rows even. Decrease 1 stitch on each side of the center neck on next row, and then every following 6th row 2 times, every 4th row 3 times, every other row 21 (23, 25, 27) times. At the same time, when piece measures 2 (2¼, 2½, 2¾)"[5 (6, 6.5, 7)cm] above casing, decrease for armhole.

Armhole Shaping Bind off 7 (7, 8, 9) stitches at the beginning of the next two rows. Decrease 1 stitch at the beginning and end of every other row 6 times. Work even on remaining 6 stitches each side until the piece measures 14 (14, 14½, 14½)"[35.5 (35.5, 37, 37)cm] from the bottom edge of the casing. Bind off.

THIS IS ONE WICKEDLY SEXY MESH

NIGHTGOWN—YOU BAD GIRL!

FRONT

Work as for the back until piece measures 37"[94cm] from the beginning.

Divide for Front

NEXT ROW (RS) Work in pattern over the next 42 (44, 46, 48) stitches, join a 2nd ball of yarn, work in pattern over remaining 42 (44, 46, 48) stitches. Work both sides even until piece measures 47"[119.5cm] from the beginning.

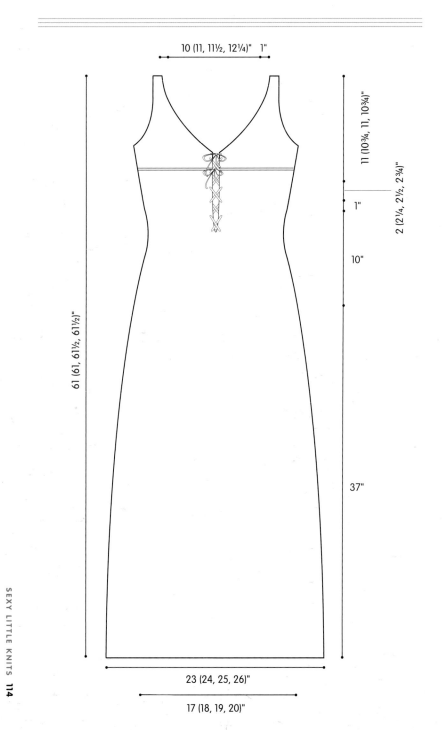

10 (11, 11½, 12¼)"   1"

11 (10¾, 11, 10¾)"

2 (2¼, 2½, 2¾)"

1"

10"

37"

61 (61, 61½, 61½)"

23 (24, 25, 26)"

17 (18, 19, 20)"

NEXT ROW (RS) (Place a marker at the beginning and end of row.) Increase 5 (5, 6, 7) stitches evenly across each half of row—47 (49, 52, 55) stitches each side. Work casings on both sides of front as for back over each 47 (49, 52, 55) stitches. Work even in stockinette stitch until piece measures 1¾ (2, 2¼, 2½)"[5 (6, 6.5, 7)cm] above casing, work buttonholes.

LEFT FRONT BUTTONHOLE ROW (RS) Knit 43 (45, 48, 51) stitches, knit 2 together, yarn over, knit 2.

RIGHT FRONT BUTTONHOLE ROW (RS) Knit 2, yarn over, (slip, slip, knit), knit 43 (45, 48, 51) stitches. Work until piece measures the same as for the back to armhole.

Armhole and Neck Shaping Work armhole shaping as for back. At the same time, decrease 1 stitch at each neck edge on next row, then every 4th row 2 times, every other row 25 (27, 29, 31) times. Work even until front measures same as the back on remaining 6 stitches each side. Bind off.

FINISHING

Block pieces. Sew the shoulder seams. Sew the side seams, leaving casing free. Sew casing openings at side seam on wrong side. With crochet hook, work 1 row of single crochet around neck and armhole edges.

Center Front Drawstring With hook, crochet a chain until it measures 50"[127cm]. Turn. Work slip stitch along length of chain. Fasten off. Lace drawstring through mesh of fronts and through buttonholes.

Waist Drawstring With hook, crochet a chain until it measures 54 (56, 58, 60)"[137 (142, 147, 152)cm]. Turn. Work slip stitch along length of chain. Fasten off. Thread drawstring through casing.

SEXPOT CAMI

Sizes
To fit S (M, L)

Finished Measurements
Bust to fit 34 (36, 38)"[86 (91.5, 96.5cm)]

Materials
▥ 4 [4, 5] 1³/₄oz/50g 540yds/500m balls of Karabella Lace Mohair (61% Super Kid Mohair, 31% Polyester, 8% Wool) in #3217 Fuchsia (MC) and 1 ball each in #3170 Light Green (A), #3223 White (B), and #3214 Yellow (C)

▥ One pair each sizes 5 [3.75mm] and 13 [9mm] knitting needles

▥ One size F/5 [3.75mm] crochet hook

▥ Cable needle

▥ 1 yd[1m] of ¼"[6mm] nylon swimwear elastic

▥ Stitch holder

Gauges
23 stitches x 32 rows = 4 x 4"[10 x 10cm] with yarn doubled and size 5 needles over stockinette stitch
12 stitches x 16 rows = 4 x 4"[10 x 10cm] with one strand of yarn and size 13 needles over bubble stitch

This vixenish fuchsia camisole features open-lace bubble stitch and picot eyelet trim that's fairly easy to do. The front features intarsia color cable sections and a simple self-finishing drawstring. A pleated flounce completes this killer '60s-inspired top.

6-STITCH LEFT CABLE
Slip next 3 stitches to cable needle and hold to the front of work, knit 3, knit 3 stitches from the cable needle.

PICOT TRIM
ROWS 1 AND 3 (WS) Purl.

ROW 2 (RS) Knit.

ROW 4 (RS) Knit 1,*yarn over, knit 2 together, repeat from * to end. Work rows 1 through 4 for picot trim.

BUBBLE STITCH
ROWS 1 AND 3 (RS) Knit.

ROW 2 Purl 1 (edge stitch), knit 1, *keeping yarn in back, slip next stitch purlwise, knit 1* repeat from * to *, end with purl 1 (edge stitch).

ROW 4 Purl 1 (edge stitch), keeping yarn in back, slip next stitch purlwise, *knit 1, keeping yarn in back slip next stitch purlwise*, repeat from * to *, end with purl 1 (edge stitch). Repeat rows 1 through 4 for bubble stitch.

BOTTOM PLEATED FLOUNCE
With smaller needles and 1 strand of MC, cast on 231 (243, 255) stitches. Work picot trim.

NEXT ROW (RS) Knit and decrease 126 (132, 138) stitches evenly—105 (111, 117) stitches. Change to larger needles. Purl next row. Work in bubble stitch pattern for 30 (32, 34) rows. Bind off loosely.

BODICE
With smaller needles and MC (double strand of yarn), cast on 94 (100, 106) stitches, work 2 rows in stockinette stitch.

SETUP ROW FOR INTARSIA CABLES Work 4 (7, 10) stitches in MC, 6 stitches in C (twist yarn between each color change to avoid holes), 14 stitches in MC, 6 stitches in B, 14 stitches in MC, 6 stitches in A, 14 stitches in MC, 6 stitches in C, 14 stitches in MC, 6 stitches in B, work 4 (7, 10) stitches in MC. Work 3 rows even.

NEXT ROW (RS) Work 6-stitch cable over each of 5 intarsia sections. Work 5 rows even.

Continue in MC only, work 6 rows even across all stitches.

Divide for Cups

NEXT ROW (RS) Work 46 (49, 52) stitches for first cup, place remaining stitches on holder for second cup. Work 1 row even. Decrease 1 stitch at the beginning and end of every 10th row once, every 6th row once, every other row 8 times, every row 8 times—10 (13, 16) stitches.

NEXT (DECREASE) ROW Knit 2 together 5 (1, 1) time(s), knit 3 together 0 (3, 4) times, knit 2 together 0 (1, 1) time—5 (5, 6) stitches.

Strap Work 10 rows of each color in this order: MC, A, MC, B, MC, C, MC, A, MC. Bind off.

For second cup, bind off center 2 stitches. Work same as first cup.

Side Straps With RS facing and 2 strands of MC, pick up and knit 12 stitches along first 2"[5cm] of side edge of cup, beginning at bottom edge. *Work 12 rows in MC across all stitches. Work 3 stitches in MC, 6 stitches in A, 3 stitches in MC. Work 3 rows even.

NEXT ROW (RS) Work 6-stitch cable over intarsia section. Work 4 rows even. Repeat from

*5 more times along length of strap, working B, C, A, B, C along length of strap for intarsia sections. Work 12 rows even in MC. Bind off.

FINISHING

Do not block pieces. Fold picot trim in half to wrong side andd sew in place. Fold bottom flounce in half and pin 3" to 4"[7.5 to 10cm] from center. Open bodice flat and flatten the center box pleat. Pin to the cups and 5"[12.5cm] of side straps. Adjust fit if necessary. Sew the flounce in place.

Inside Casing With WS facing, in MC and smaller needles, pick up and knit 94 (100, 106) stitches evenly across inside edge above last intarsia row. Work 4 rows in stockinette stitch. Bind off. Sew casing to inside top.

Edgings With 1 strand of yarn, work 2 rows of single crochet around all edges of straps and bra cups as follows:

STRAPS First row B, second row MC.

OUTSIDE EDGES OF CUPS First row B, second row A.

CENTER EDGES OF CUPS First row A, second row C.

Insert a 16 (17, 18)"[40.5 (43, 46)cm] length of elastic into casing and secure the ends.

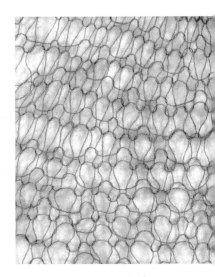

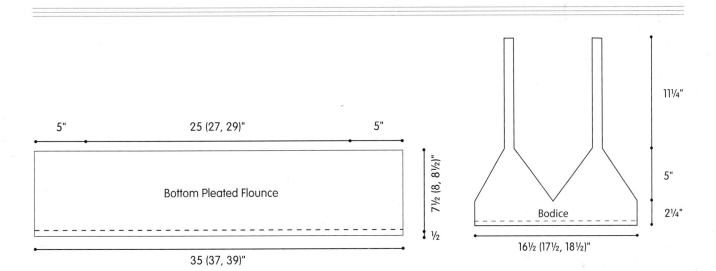

5"   25 (27, 29)"   5"

Bottom Pleated Flounce

35 (37, 39)"

7½ (8, 8½)"   ½

11¼"

Bodice

5"

2¼"

16½ (17½, 18½)"

SEXPOT BOTTOM

Sizes
To fit S (M, L)

Finished Measurements
Hip 32 (36, 40)"[81 (91.5, 101.5)cm]

Materials
▨ 2 (3, 3) 1³⁄₄oz/50g 540yds/500m balls of Karabella Lace Mohair (61% Super Kid Mohair, 31% Polyester, 8% Wool) in #3217 Pink (MC) and 1 ball each in #3170 Light Green (A), #3223 White (B), and #3214 Yellow (C)

▨ One pair size 5 [3.75mm] knitting needles

▨ One size F/5 [3.75mm] crochet hook

▨ Cable needle

▨ 2¹⁄₂yds[2.25m] of ¹⁄₄"[6mm] nylon swimwear elastic

Gauge
23 stitches x 32 rows = 4 x 4"[10 x 10cm] on size 5 needles over stockinette stitch

I love these vintage colors and cute cable stitching. Full-bottom panty styles are super retro and comfy. Try this style in a silk yarn for a more sophisticated look, or try cotton for a more wearable casual style. Knit the panties in stockinette and cable knit with crochet elastic waist and leg openings. Follow the top for intarsia instructions, twist different color yarns together to avoid holes.

6-STITCH LEFT CABLE
Slip next 3 stitches to cable needle and hold to the front of work, knit 3, knit 3 stitches from cable needle.

FRONT
Cast on 12 stitches in MC. Begin with a WS row, work in stockinette stitch for 21 rows. Increase 2 stitches at beginning and end of every row 8 times, then every other row 3 times. Cast on 3 stitches at beginning of next 12 (8, 8) rows—92 (80, 80) stitches. Cast on 0 (6, 9) stitches at beginning of next 0 (4, 4) rows—92 (104, 116) stitches. Work even for 5 row:

Setup Row for Intarsia Cables
ROW 1 (RS) Knit 9 (15, 21) stitches in MC, 6 stitches in C, 11 stitches in MC, 6 stitches in B, 11 stitches in MC, 6 stitches in A, 11 stitches in MC, 6 stitches in B, 11 stitches in MC, 6 stitches in C, knit 9 (15, 21) stitches in MC.

Work 1 row even, twisting yarn between color changes to avoid holes.

NEXT ROW (RS) Work 6-stitch left cable across all 5 intarsia sections. Work 7 rows even in intarsia. Repeat the last 8 rows 3 times more.

NEXT ROW (RS) Work 6-stitch left cable across all 5 intarsia sections. Work 2 rows even, ending with a RS row.

NEXT ROW (WS) Purl in MC across all stitches of next row.

NEXT ROW (RS) Work 4 (6, 8) rows even, bind off.

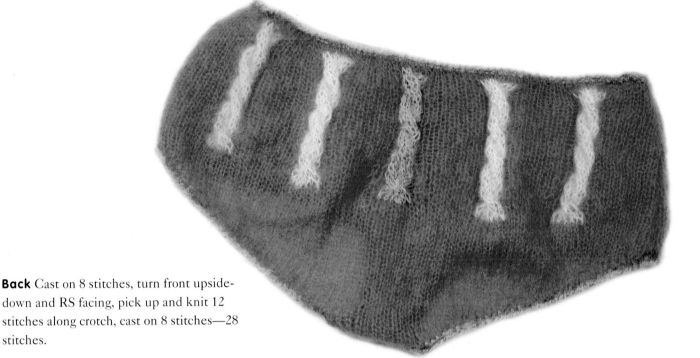

Back Cast on 8 stitches, turn front upside-down and RS facing, pick up and knit 12 stitches along crotch, cast on 8 stitches—28 stitches.

NEXT ROW (WS) Work even. Cast on 24 stitches at the beginning of the next 2 rows, and cast on 8 (14, 20) stitches at the beginning of the next 2 rows—92 (104, 116) stitches. Work 5 rows even.

NEXT ROW (RS) Work as for the front, beginning with setup for intarsia cables row until end. Bind off.

FINISHING

Do not block. Sew the side seams. In A, work 1 row of reverse single crochet around leg openings and across top waist, carrying elastic. Secure ends.

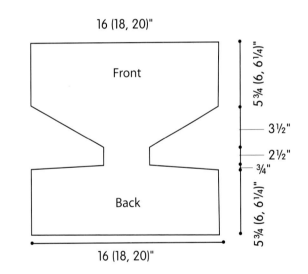

16 (18, 20)"

Front

5¾ (6, 6¼)"

3½"

2½"

¾"

Back

5¾ (6, 6¼)"

16 (18, 20)"

Cute '60s-style bottoms are back in fashion. Thongs are out, thankfully. Have fun experimenting with different lace stitches or even cute polka dots.

For a casual, wearable style, try a cool cotton with Fixation yarn for the banding. For a mature, sultry look, go for an exotic silk yarn with peek-a-boo stitching. Make an assortment of these and you'll be glad you did.

ABOUT THE AUTHOR

Ashley Paige talks about becoming a knitwear designer,
finding inspiration, and flaunting it.

MAKING IT BIG WITH LITTLE KNITS

I kinda fell into the knitwear business when I
started my knit bikini line. I wanted to create a
swimwear line that was unique and had little
competition. I had this beautiful knit bikini I had
scored at a thrift store years ago. When I was
beginning to come up with ideas for the swim line,
I came across the bikini and the idea popped into
my head to do an entire collection of knit bikinis.
Thus, the knitwear designer was born. I was in
the forefront of this reemerging trend, but didn't
really know it at the time. I guess that's what they
mean when they say timing is everything! Now I
offer dresses, tops, and even accessories, including socks, hats, and handbags—all knit!

The Birth of the First Ashley Paige Bikini

My interest in beachwear began when I was a
kid. I grew up in Pensacola, Florida, and spent
most of my time in a bathing suit—sailing,
swimming, and hanging out on the beach.

I got my first big break when I decided to design
a small group of knit bikinis in 2000 and took my
collection to the swimwear trade show in Miami.
Sports Illustrated loved the designs, and one of
my suits was featured in SI. It made the cover of
the magazine's 2003 swimsuit edition, and it was
incorporated into the packaging of the
magazine's DVD. After that, the orders started
flowing in, and we were off and running.

So far, my career has led me down some
interesting paths, searching for the perfect way to
construct a water-friendly, knit bikini. The journey

has taken me to Hong Kong, Paris, and Brazil—
all for one little bikini.

INSPIRATION: FROM THE DRAWING BOARD TO THE SURFBOARD

I never pinpoint exactly where my inspiration
comes from because it comes from so many
different things. It could be someone walking
down the street with attitude, or a passionate
song, a movie, or just some memories from my
past. Sometimes a great fabric or yarn can be the
single inspiration.

Some of my favorite designers are Sonia Rykiel,
a fabulous French knitwear designer, and Marc
Jacobs, the great American sportswear designer.

Once I get an idea from something inspiring,
I sketch the design on paper, make the first
prototype, and then do a fitting on a fit model.
Then I make a few changes and finalize the fit
and design. Then it's onto sales and production.

Seventies Forever

I would say my design sense is organic, simple,
fun, and, oh, let's not forget sexy!

A lot of that design sense comes from the
seventies. I love the seventies! I was born in 1970,
and I'm also a nature-loving, hippie-girl at heart.
That's just the look that appeals to me, and
anything handmade reminds me of my family
and my childhood. I am very sentimental.

BIKINIS FOR EVERY BODY

The beautiful thing about a knit bikini is how truly

forgiving it is. A knit will actually stretch and mold to the shape of your body, without gripping like a traditional lycra with tight elastic banding. So, with a knit bikini, I don't believe there's a wrong way to wear it—it's more about your attitude and spirit that makes the bikini unique to you. You should choose a bikini you feel comfortable in. Some of the most fashionable women are the ones who go against the grain and wear what they want with confidence.

Of course, there are some basic rules to consider:

- If you're short, you may want to choose a bikini that ties higher on your hips to make your legs look longer and leaner.
- If you're tall, a low-rider bikini with a boy-cut bottom will give you a little extra-sexy proportion.
- If you have a large chest, halter tops are great, while a strapless top may be less comfortable for you.
- A bandeau style is a truly high-fashion look and it is fabulous for small-bosomed women.
- All these rules about fit and shape apply to a one-piece as well.

What is Sexy?

Sexy is showing off your best assets in flirtatious ways. Example: If you have great legs, show them and you will feel sexy. If you have great eyes, use a little smoky eyeliner and see the reactions you get. I have a curvy body shape, and I show it off with form-fitting clothes when I want to look and feel sexy.

Everyone is different, but if you know what part of you is sexy and you flaunt it, it is impossible not to feel sexy.

BEYOND-BIKINI AMBITIONS

So far, I have lent my name and persona to support philanthropic efforts benefiting cancer awareness, the Humane Society, and homeless children around the world. I would love to build my company into one of the leading fashion knitwear companies and use our advertisements to promote socially and environmentally responsible causes.

Ashley swimming with her dad off the coast of Florida.

YARN RESOURCES

The yarns used in this book are widely available at fine yarn stores everywhere. We've offered this guide as a resource for locating the store nearest you. Each of the websites listed offers a store locator so that it's easy and convenient to find a place that sells the yarn you want. Many of the websites will also allow you to place online orders. For information on substituting yarns, please see page 16.

ANNY BLATT
annyblatt.com
(248) 486-6160
7796 Boardwalk
Brighton MI, 48116

BERROCO YARNS
(800) 343-4948
berroco.com/yarn_shops.html

CASCADE YARNS
cascadeyarns.com
sales@cascadeyarn.com

DIAKEITO YARN
dancingfibers.com/retailers.html

DEBBIE BLISS YARNS
debbieblissonline.com

GGH YARNS
Muench Yarns, Inc.
 (800)733-9276
www.muenchyarns.com

HEMP FOR KNITTING
hempforknitting.com/usstores.htm

KAALUND YARNS
kaalundyarns.com.au

KARABELLA YARNS
(212) 684-2665
www.karabellayarns.com

LANA GROSSA
lanagrossa.com

WENDY VELVET TOUCH
is distributed exclusively in the Unites States by Berroco.
http://www.tbramsden.co.uk/html/links.html

INDEX